ACKNOWLEDGMENTS

The authors gratefully acknowledge the many contributions of time and resources made by those who collaborated on the creation of the 2011 edition of the KW Market Navigator.

A special thanks to all Keller Williams associates who took the time to share their experiences in the KW research surveys.

This resource represents the culmination of a year's worth of research studies conducted by the KW Research Department. The team designs the studies, orchestrates the survey process, collects the data, evaluates the results, and interprets the findings that are most relevant for associates in the field.

Once the data have been collated and analyzed, talented graphic designers and writers transform the numbers into a collection of compelling infographics that are easy to grasp and fun to read.

METHODOLOGY

The findings presented were compiled from a series of large-scale surveys administered by the KW Research Department to all Keller Williams associates in North America.

- Lead Generation Survey: 2,417 respondents (April 2010)
- Home Buyers Survey: 3,528 respondents (May 2010)
- Green Survey: 1,769 respondents (July 2010)
- Home Sellers Survey: 4,073 respondents (November 2009)

Thanks in advance for your participation in future surveys!

NOTICES

While Keller Williams Realty, Inc. (KWRI) has taken due care in the preparation of all materials in this product, we do not guarantee their accuracy. KWRI makes no warranties either expressed or implied with regard to the information and programs presented in this product.

All materials are copyright © 2011 Keller Williams Realty, Inc. All rights reserved.

Printed March 2011.

No part of this publication and its associated materials may be reproduced or transmitted in any form or by any means without the prior written permission of Keller Williams Realty, Inc.

Table of Contents

VISION - U.S. 1

Economic Snapshot - U.S. 3

The 5 U.S. Statistics 4

- Home Sales Stabilize 4
- Home Prices Stabilize 4
- Market Inventory: Homes on the Shelf 5
- Mortgage Rates at Historical Lows 6
- More Bang for Your Buck: Homes Are More Affordable 7

Events That Drive the Numbers - U.S. 8

- Available Sides Per Agent Remain Steady 8
- Uncertainty About Economic Outlook 9
- Shadow Inventory Looms 9
- Mortgage Rates Held Low 9
- Extended Home Buyer Tax Credit Boosted Demand in the First Half of 2010 10

Commercial Real Estate - U.S. 11

- Vacancy Rates Remain High 11
- New Commercial Loans Plummet and Delinquency Rates Rise 12
- Lend, Extend, Pretend, Suspend 13
- Opportunities 14

Luxury Real Estate - U.S. 15

- Supply of Inventory 15
- Days on Market 16
- Original Price-to-Sell Ratio 16
- Opportunity in the Luxury Market 17

What the U.S. Government Is Doing 18

Started: Second Round of Fed's Monetary Stimulus 18
Extended: Income Tax Cuts 18
Extended: Conforming Loan Limits 19
Halted: New Mortgage Disclosure Rule 19

VISION - CANADA 20

Economic Snapshot - Canada 23

5 Canadian Statistics 24

Home Sales Cool 24
Home Prices Continue Upward Trend 25
Inventory Stabilizes 26
Mortgage Rates 27
Affordability Improves Slightly 27

Events That Drive the Numbers - Canada 28

Canada's Monetary Stimulus Continues to Boost the Market 28
Implementation of New, Tighter Mortgage Rules 28
Improving Credit Market 29
Available Sides Per Agent 29
Strong Currency 29

What the Canadian Government Is Doing 30

Agreement Reached Between Competition Bureau and CREA 30
Tightening Mortgage Regulations 30

Commercial Real Estate - Canada 31

Vacancy Rates Remain Steady 31

VISION - PERSPECTIVE AND ACTION ... 32

How Do We Recover? ... 35
The 4 Gears of Success ... 36

HOME BUYERS ... 40

Now's the Time to Buy ... 42
Mortgage Rates Reach Record Lows ... 42
Home Prices Stabilize ... 43
Affordability at Record Levels ... 43
Home Buyers' Relationship Status ... 44
Average Age of Home Buyers ... 44
Type of Home Purchased ... 45
Price Is the Most Important Factor for Buyers ... 46
Why Buyers Buy ... 46
Location Preferences ... 47
Length of Buyer Consultation ... 48
Buyer Consultation ... 49
Time-Saving Tips ... 49
Tax Credit ... 50
Buyer Qualification ... 50
Going Green: Top Five Green Features ... 51
Interest in Green Features ... 51

FIRST-TIME HOME BUYERS 52

    Marital Status of First-Time Home Buyers..54

    Family Makeup of First-Time Home Buyers..55

    Generation X and Y 55

    Preferences Among First-Time Buyers 56

    Average Beds/Baths 56

    Interest in Nontraditional Transactions 57

    Home-Buying Criteria 58

    Key Triggers 59

    Key Activities Prior to Home Tours...60

    Most First-Time Home Buyer Consultations Lasted 30 Mins.–1 Hr........61

    Percentage of Agents Who Do a First-Time Home Buyer Consultation 61

    Most Had an Accepted Offer Within Three Days of Submission..................61

HOME SELLERS 62

    Features That Attract Buyers..65

    What's Selling 66

    Top Nine Reasons Sellers Sell 66

    Shipshape Sells 67

    Most Common Updates 67

    Condition Is Key 68

    Condition: Better Is Better 69

    Curb Appeal...70

    Strategic Staging...71

    Staging 72

    Who Staged? 72

    Top Ten Pricing Considerations 73

    Impact of Pricing to Sell..73

    When Marketing the Listing...74

    Closing Costs 75

    Speed of the Sale 75

DISTRESSED PROPERTIES..76

    Agent Involvement..78

    Motivating Factors..78

    Agents' Key Challenges With Distressed Properties 79

    Common Short Sale Scenarios 80

    The Downward Spiral of Defaults and Home Prices 81

    Counsel Patience for Your Distressed Property Buyers 83

    Early Stage "SOS" to Lender 83

    Lag Time in Contacting Lender 84

    Lender Recourse: Deficiency Judgment 85

    Assessing Risk of Lender Seeking Deficiency Judgment.................85

    Distressed Property Sales Success Factors 86

    Short Sale Checklist 87

    Typical Distressed Property Time Line 88

GREEN IS THE NEW GOLD..90

    1 in 10 Associates Now Position Themselves as Green Specialists.................92

    Green Knowledge 92

    Green Value 92

    What Buyers Want: Three Green Buckets 93

    Tap into Our Green Community 93

    Top Three Reasons Home Buyers Want Green Features................94

    Green Availability 94

    Green Prices 94

    From the Agent Perspective:
    Who Values Green Features the Most?..95

    Fewer Days on the Market...95

    Green Grows 95

    Green Is Not a Fad..96

    Green Features Buyers Look for Most 96

    Green Keys to Success 97

    Seize the Opportunity: Specialized Training..................................97

LEAD GENERATION..98

    Goals for Weekly Contacts 100

    How Much Time Do You Block Each Week? 101

    Lead Generation Time Blocking...101

    Use of Traditional Lead Generation Sources................................102

    Communication Preferences 102

    Texting Is the New Email 103

    Top Three Prospecting-Based Lead Sources................................104

    Top Three Lead Sources 105

    Top Three Technology-Based Lead Sources 105

    Met Database 106

    Haven't Met Database 106

    Attracting Website Leads 107

    Capturing Website Leads 108

MAIN POINTS...110

    Top 12 Takeaways 112

INTRODUCTION

How's business?

I am continually asked this question by literally thousands of real estate professionals. The fact is, it's all a matter of how you look at it.

It's easy, of course, to confuse market conditions with market opportunities. The truth is that the state of the market only tells you how to succeed—not whether you will. What is productive is to view the real estate market from every angle, study the big picture, size up your opportunity, and then seize it.

The KW Market Navigator was created to help informed, forward-thinking real estate professionals to sharpen their understanding of the critical interactions that are at play within the real estate market. My hope is that it helps you to keep your sights high and field of vision wide, and in doing so, you help an increasing number of clients to navigate the shifting market.

The market is what you make of it. Nothing more. Nothing less.

ONWARD ...

Gary Keller

For other resources and to purchase additional copies of KW Market Navigator: Vision and Opportunities 2011, *please go to* kwu.kw.com/marketnavigator.

Vision - U.S.

Economic Snapshot - U.S. 3
The 5 U.S. Statistics 4
   1. Home Sales Stabilize 4
   2. Home Prices Stabilize 4
   3. Market Inventory: Homes on the Shelf 5
   4. Mortgage Rates at Historical Lows 6
   5. More Bang for Your Buck: Homes Are More Affordable 7
Events That Drive the Numbers - U.S. 8
   1. Available Sides Per Agent Remain Steady 8
   2. Uncertainty About Economic Outlook 9
   3. Shadow Inventory Looms 9
   4. Mortgage Rates Held Low 9
   5. Extended Home Buyer Tax Credit Boosted Demand
      in the First Half of 2010 10
Commercial Real Estate - U.S. 11
   Vacancy Rates Remain High 11
   New Commercial Loans Plummet
   and Delinquency Rates Rise 12
   Lend, Extend, Pretend, Suspend 13
   Opportunities 14
Luxury Real Estate – U.S. 15
   Supply of Inventory 15
   Days on Market 16
   Original Price-to-Sell Ratio 16
   Opportunity in the Luxury Market 17
What the U.S. Government Is Doing 18
   Started: Second Round of Fed's Monetary Stimulus 18
   Extended: Income Tax Cuts 18
   Extended: Conforming Loan Limits 19
   Halted: New Mortgage Disclosure Rules 19

Economic Snapshot - U.S.

The economic health of the United States can be revealed through three markers: *gross domestic product (GDP)*, *inflation*, and *unemployment*.

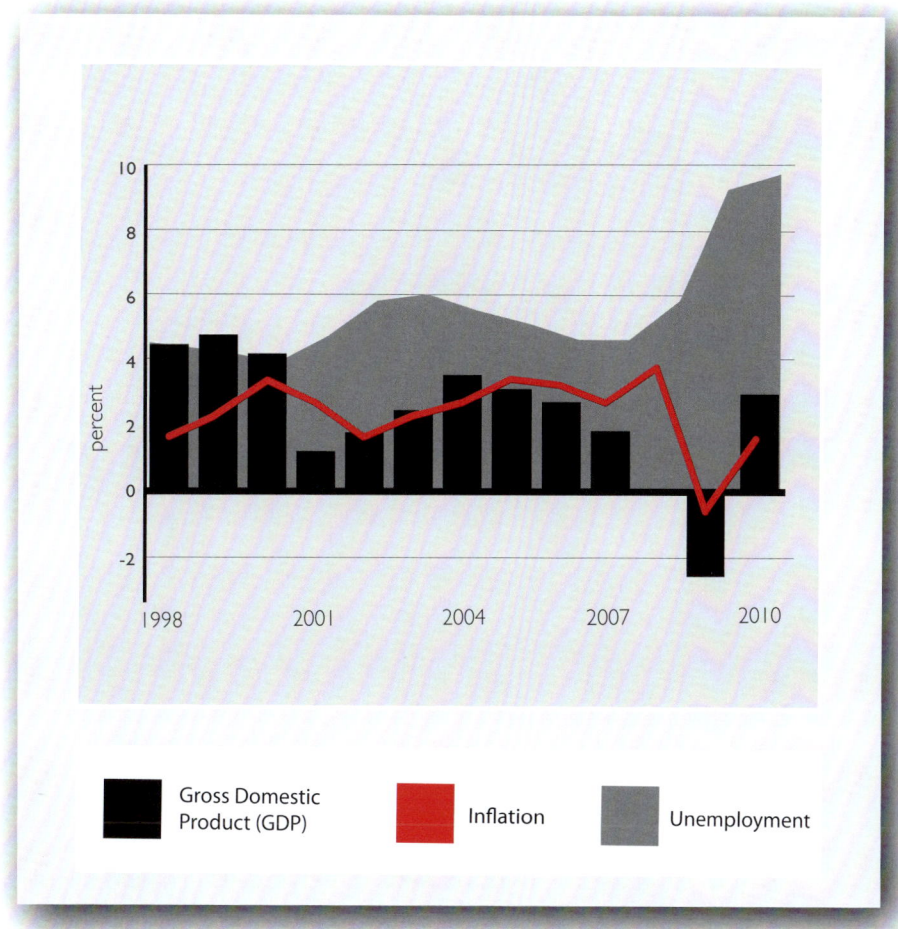

GDP

The market value of goods and services produced by labor and property. Early in 2010, the U.S. economy continued to build on the strong momentum experienced in the second half of 2009. While the expansion slowed on average, the economy has posted stronger performance in recent months, led by stronger-than-expected consumer spending and strong exports.

Inflation

The average change in prices of goods and services as measured by the consumer price index (CPI). Inflation returned to a more typical level after dipping into deflationary territory in 2009, averaging around 1.6% in 2010.

Unemployment

Unemployment dropped from 9.9% in 2009 to 9.4% in the final month of 2010, and recent economic reports are showing some renewed vigor in economic activity. The tax package reached in December is expected to boost demand and spur hiring in 2011, resulting in a slow decline in the unemployment rate which remains high by historical standards.

KW MARKET NAVIGATOR 2011

The 5 U.S. Statistics

Every Agent Should Know

The housing market is both a driver and a reflection of what is happening in the U.S. economy. Keep this information at your fingertips as you inform and advise your clients on what is happening in the market.

1 HOME SALES STABILIZE

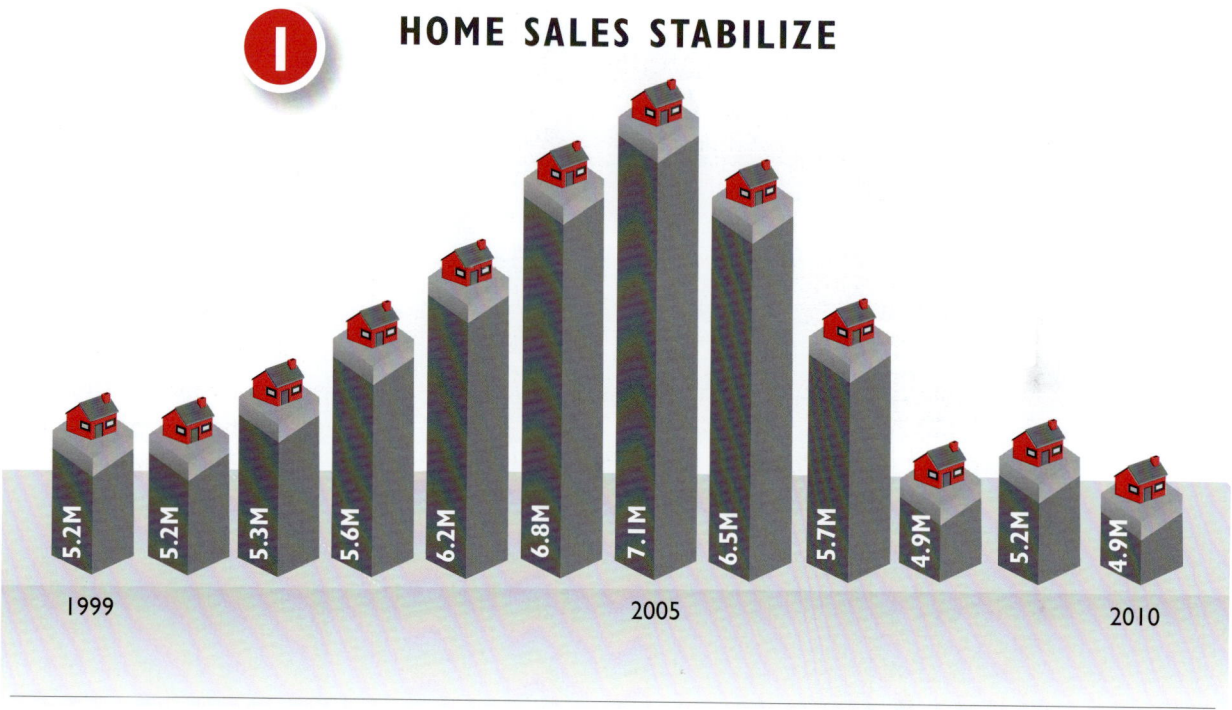

1999: 5.2M, 5.2M, 5.3M, 5.6M, 6.2M, 6.8M, 7.1M (2005), 6.5M, 5.7M, 4.9M, 5.2M, 4.9M (2010)

2 HOME PRICES STABILIZE
for the first time since 2006

2008: $198K
2009: $172.5K (−13%)
2010: $173K (+.3%)

The median home price increased slightly by 0.3% in 2010: the first annual price gain since 2006, as buyer incentives and record affordability helped boost sales and stabilize home prices. The foreclosure freeze resulting from the robo-signing scandal in October has also contributed to firming home prices. There were fewer foreclosure sales, which sold for an average 28% discount compared to nonforeclosure sales during 2010.

VISION

③ MARKET INVENTORY: HOMES ON THE SHELF

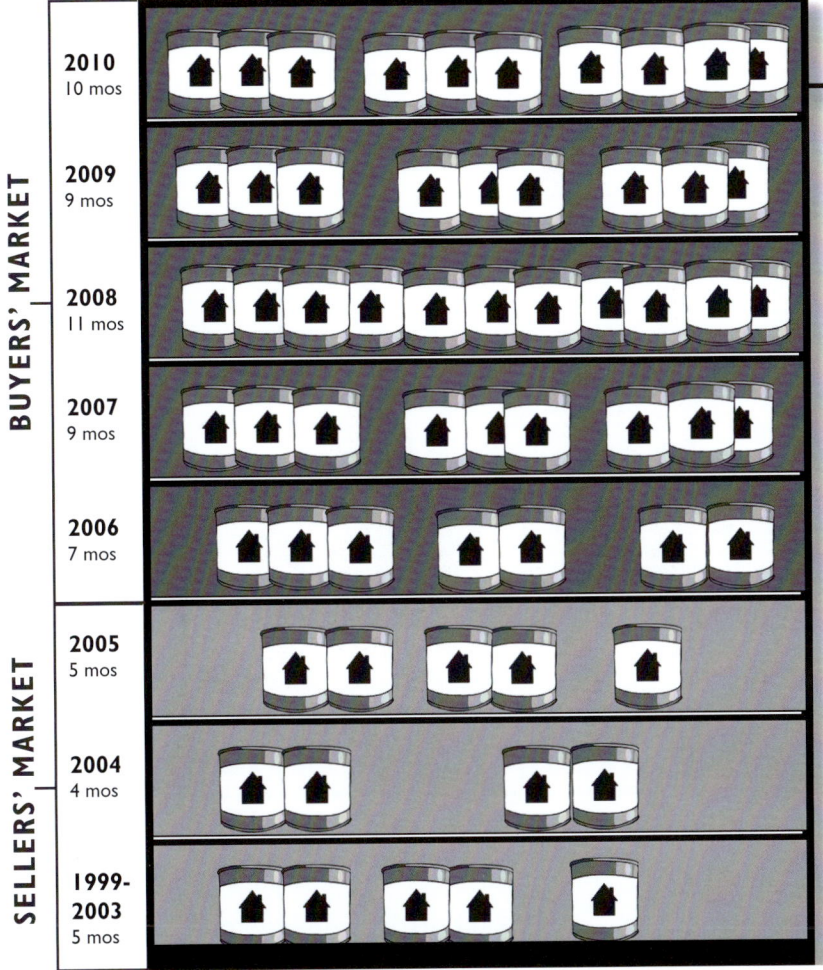

> **Sale prices good only while stocks last!**
>
> **All reasonable offers will be considered!**
>
> While the average inventory for all of 2010 was 9.4 months, it has been steadily declining month by month since peaking in July, standing at **8.2 months in December.**

> *It's our job to know these numbers. Our clients aren't paying us to stick a sign in their yard, they are paying us to keep them informed.*
>
> — Gary Keller

MORTGAGE RATES AT HISTORICAL LOWS
A Perspective

	1989	2010
Bread	$0.67	$2.49
Gas (gal.)	$0.97	$2.73
New Car	$15,350	$28,400
House	$94,000	$173,000
Monthly Payment	$825	$896
Mortgage Rate	**10%**	**4.69%**

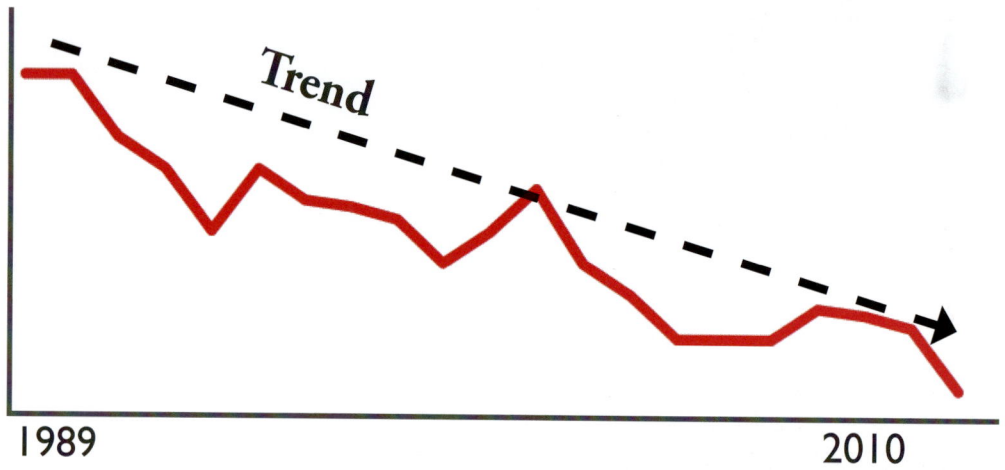

Now is the time to lock in mortgage rates, which touched bottom on November 11, 2010, at 4.17%, and averaged 4.69% for the year: an all-time low since Freddie Mac started its mortgage survey in 1971. At the end of December, rates stood at 4.71%. With rates this low, most feel they only have one direction to go—up.

MORE BANG FOR YOUR BUCK: HOMES ARE MORE AFFORDABLE
Your Housing Dollar Will Go Further Than It Ever Has Before

Affordability measures ability to buy—that is, the amount of a family's income consumed by the mortgage. In 1981 it took 36% of the family income to pay a mortgage. Today it takes 14%—a historic low!

> *It's stunning when you realize we are not doing a good enough job informing people about affordability. Every real estate agent should be walking down the street, flapping their arms, with the affordability index in one hand and amortization tables in the other. I promise you that if you do that, you will impact people's decisions and change their lives.*
>
> — Gary Keller

KW MARKET NAVIGATOR 2011

Events That Drive the Numbers - U.S.

Unprecedented factors and events in 2010 continued to shape the real estate market at the national level.

❶ AVAILABLE SIDES PER AGENT REMAIN STEADY

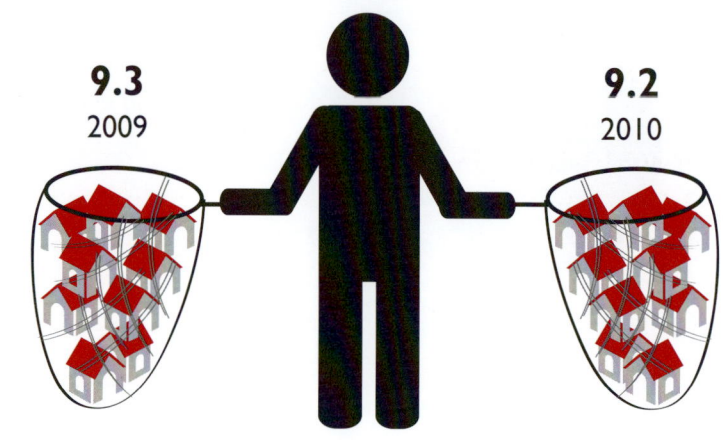

9.3 2009

9.2 2010

Sales per agent

Agent count increases, peaks, and declines

Opportunity!

1999   2004   2010

2 UNCERTAINTY ABOUT ECONOMIC OUTLOOK

Accelerated growth in the market will be held back until job and economic growth gain further traction.

Uncertainty comes from one thing: unemployment. It's a long road back. It's not going to happen overnight.

— Gary Keller

3 SHADOW INVENTORY LOOMS

The downward trend in late 2010 in foreclosure activity, which was most likely due to the fallout from the robo-signing controversy, is expected to reverse. The lingering aftereffects of the foreclosure freezes could result in an eventual glut of foreclosure sales that could prove problematic for the market.

4 MORTGAGE RATES HELD LOW

The Fed's continued support in keeping interest rates low has helped fuel demand for new mortgages. This has also helped struggling homeowners avoid default and foreclosure on their home loans by allowing them to sell, refinance, or both.

EXTENDED HOME BUYER TAX CREDIT BOOSTED DEMAND IN THE FIRST HALF OF 2010

Existing home sales resumed an upward trend since bottoming in July. As steady job creation is expected to continue, industry experts are hopeful for 2011.

We intentionally pulled home buyers from the future to keep us out of a depression, and it worked. If the government hadn't done this, home sales and home prices could have fallen off the table.

— Gary Keller

ANNUAL SALES IN MILLIONS

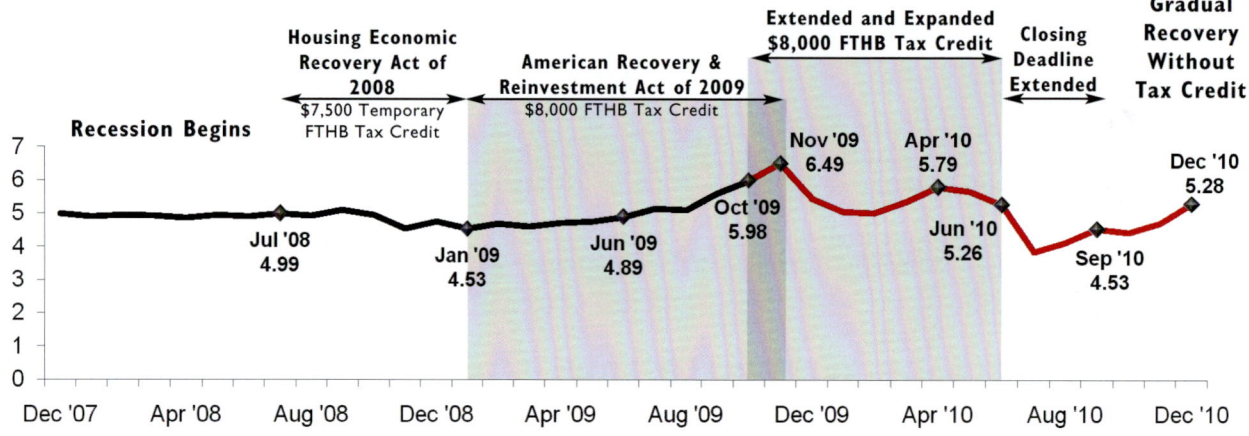

Commercial Real Estate - U.S.

The commercial real estate market historically lags closely behind the residential market. From 2008–2009, the residential market saw a decline, and then from 2009–2010, markets stabilized. Following suit, the commercial market saw substantial declines from 2009–2010. The United States has seen an increase in commercial vacancy rates almost across the board. The only signs of strength were the multifamily vacancy rates. These are considerably lower than other commercial sectors, because, as homeowners lose their homes to distressed sales, many are forced to rent for the 2–7 years it takes to repair their credit.

VACANCY RATES REMAIN HIGH
2010

Industrial	Retail	Office	Multifamily
15% Vacancy	13% Vacancy	17% Vacancy	6% Vacancy

OFFICE VACANCY

During the second half of 2010, the office rental market took a step in the right direction for the first time in more than three years, with only a slight decline in vacancy rates. Historically, 13%–14% is the equilibrium rate for office vacancy, which means before rents can start climbing, vacancies must remain at or below this rate. Industry consensus is that, with the slow recovery in the job market, it could be approximately 2–3 years before vacancies reach equilibrium again.

NEW COMMERCIAL LOANS PLUMMET AND DELINQUENCY RATES RISE

Like the residential market, the connection between delinquency rates and price has a substantial impact on the market. As more businesses downsize and vacancies rise, it becomes harder for landlords to service their loans, leading to higher delinquencies. As delinquencies rise, distressed sales increase and prices decline; as prices fall, borrowers have less motivation to make payments on their underwater property, fueling the cycle further.

There's no money, so there is no new development. This will allow demand to catch up with supply.

— Buddy Norman

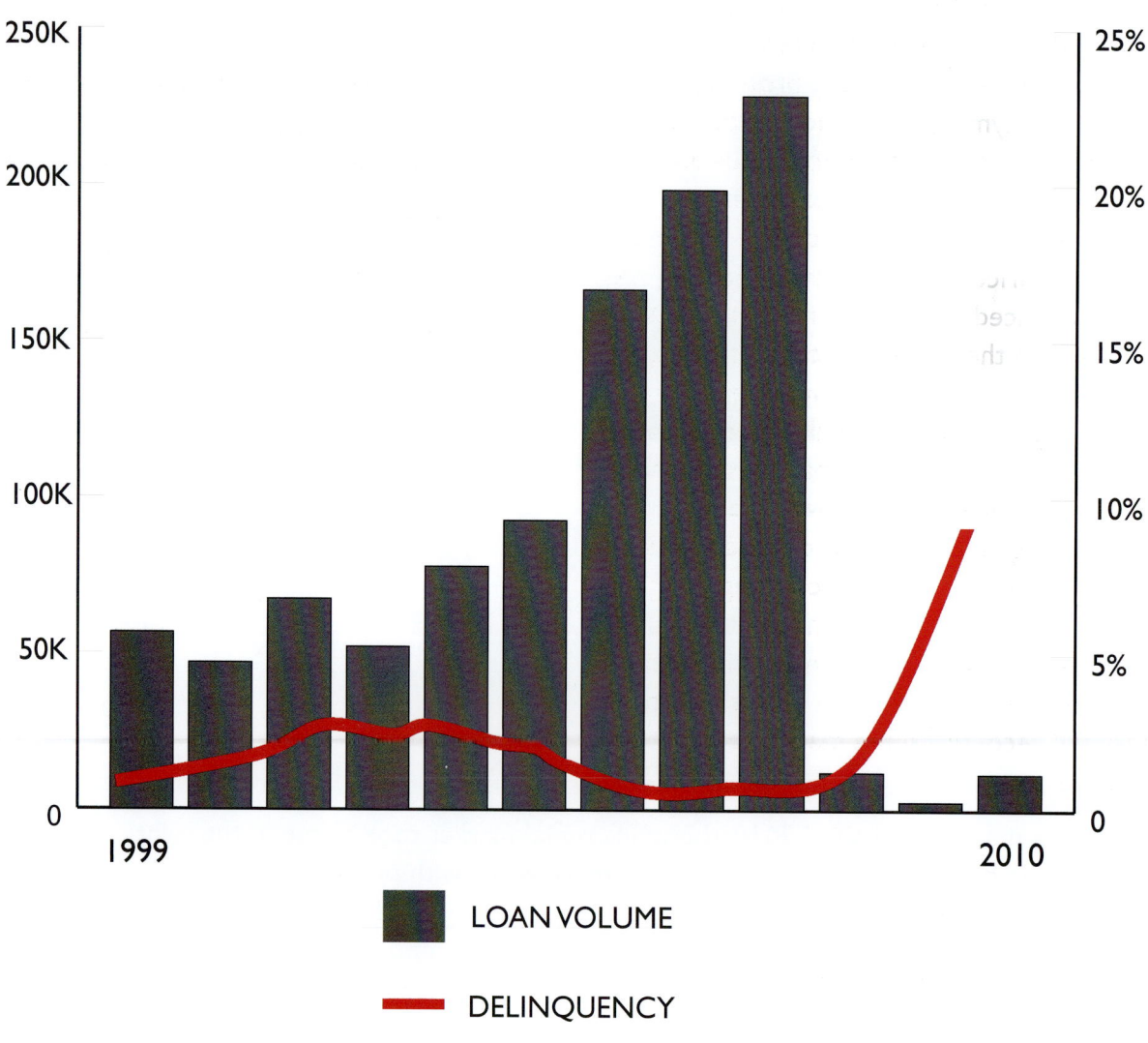

LEND, EXTEND, PRETEND, SUSPEND

To avoid losing money on foreclosures, lenders over the past two years have undertaken a strategy of "extending and pretending"—as long as the property owner is making payments, the lender proceeds as if the property has not lost value and extends the terms of the loan using cost accounting, which is based on the property's purchase price. In 2011, cost accounting was to be replaced by mark-to-market, which is based on the property's current value. This would have created a new sense of realism for the banks and likely would have resulted in amending the loans rather than just extending them. However, the Financial Accounting Standards Board passed a rule that banks could continue carrying their loans at cost for the remainder of 2011. Many believe that by suspending the pain of putting those losses on the books, healing and real recovery in the market is being delayed.

> *The Fed allowed cost accounting. Banks are keeping losses off the books, carrying loans forward until appreciation bails them out. They call them "zombie loans." They are playing a shell game. It makes it exceedingly challenging to deal with the commercial sector.*
>
> — Buddy Norman

OPPORTUNITIES

1. **Distressed Properties.** These often come with substantial discounts and, when under-valued, represent opportunities for buyers looking to get a good deal, just like residential properties.

2. **Quality Yield Properties.** Investment opportunities like T-bills and CDs are not as attractive to investors as quality properties in good locations with solid cash flow and cap rates.

3. **Tenant Representation.** With high vacancy rates that may be approaching a peak, there are plentiful opportunities for tenants to find a great deal on office, retail, or industrial space.

4. **Owner Occupants.** Companies that can afford to buy can find great opportunities to purchase space as both a long-term investment and a place to do business. While interest rates have started to inch back up, they remain near historical lows, helping to keep costs low.

Banks are going to be the biggest clients. They are going to need eyes and ears out in the field telling them what to do with their inventory.

— Buddy Norman

YOUR COMMERCIAL REAL ESTATE OPPORTUNITIES CHECKLIST!

- ☐ Distressed Properties
- ☐ Quality Yield Properties
- ☐ Tenant Representation
- ☐ Owner Occupants

Luxury Real Estate - U.S.

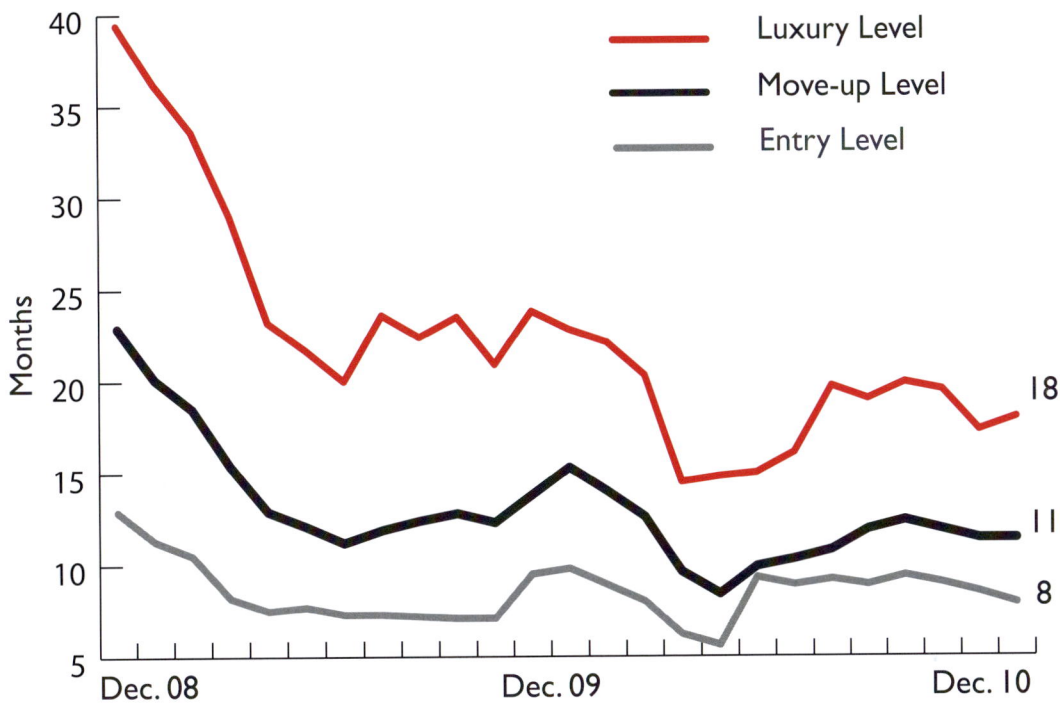

SUPPLY OF INVENTORY

Inventory for luxury markets has dropped remarkably, from an average of 40 months in December 2008 to 18 months in December 2010. Two factors contributed to the rise and subsequent fall of inventory:

- At the height of the financial crisis from late 2008 to 2009, jumbo mortgage lending essentially froze, causing inventory to rise as fewer buyers could obtain a loan. Although the situation is much improved, it is limited to those who can qualify and have the ability to make large down payments.

- Typically, the number of wealthy individuals increases or decreases depending on their level of net worth. Since 2007, these numbers have been aligned. From 2007–2008, the number of high net worth individuals declined by 27%–28%, and from 2008–2009, the number of wealthy individuals rebounded by 12%–16%, creating a larger pool of buyers with the financial wherewithal to purchase luxury homes.

DAYS ON MARKET

As the price point climbs, buyers become more and more scarce and the inventory sits for longer on the market. The minimum average days on market (DOM) for all price points is about 90 days, or 3 months, and there's still a lot of volatility above the entry level in the number of days on market.

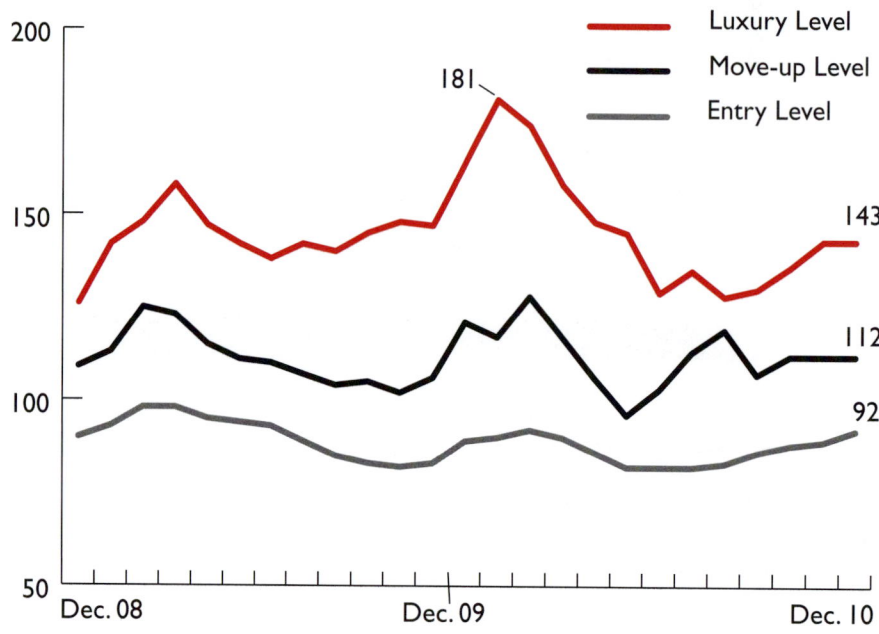

DISCOUNT FROM ORIGINAL PRICE

For the past two years, homes in the luxury market have sold for 85% list-to-sell ratio, a 15% discount from the original list price. At the height of the sellers' market, luxury homes typically sold for 97%–98% of the list price, a discount of 2%–3%. Homes under the luxury market threshold generally average a discount of 10% off the original list price.

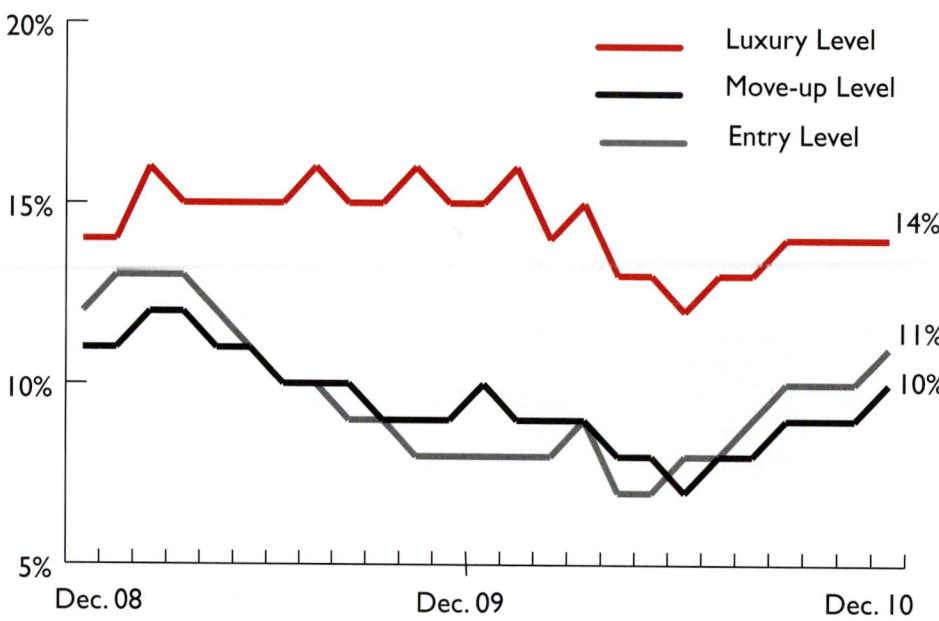

OPPORTUNITY IN THE LUXURY MARKET

> GREATER SUPPLY
> +
> LONGER DOM
> +
> GREATER DISCOUNT
> =
> OPPORTUNITY FOR:
>
> INVESTORS
> AND MOVE-UP BUYERS

1. Investors in the luxury market include both flippers and holders of undervalued properties.

Cash investors see solid investment opportunities in undervalued luxury homes. Some of these are being flipped and others are being held until the market improves.

2. Move-up buyers who were previously priced out of the luxury market get their chance.

The drop in luxury prices from the peak has made owning a luxury home more attainable for buyers with a stable job, cash for a down payment, and a good credit score. They are either using some of the more accessible jumbo loans or they have enough cash for the down payment to pull their mortgage below the jumbo level.

What the U.S. Government Is Doing

After the extensive measures taken by the government in 2009 in an attempt to correct and control the housing market and economy, in 2010 the focus was primarily on extending some tax and stimulus measures while letting go of others such as the home buyer tax credit.

STARTED:
SECOND ROUND OF FED'S MONETARY STIMULUS

Consumers and business owners alike need access to readily available money they can borrow on credit. However, after the financial crisis, this credit had essentially dried up. In order to stimulate lending, the government had allowed banks to borrow money at historically low rates under the assumption that the banks would use the money to extend credit. Unfortunately, the banks actually used this advantage to purchase guaranteed Treasury bills. In response, the Fed has spurred lending by resorting to the more unconventional tool of "quantitative easing," where they purchased bad assets from the banks and started buying Treasuries in order to lower rates even further. This increase in demand for Treasuries lowered the interest rate spread, making Treasuries less attractive investment for banks, and consumer and business lending a more attractive investment.

EXTENDED:
INCOME TAX CUTS

The current income tax rates were extended through 2013. The tax cut is expected to put more money in the pockets of families most likely to spend it, sparking demand, helping businesses to grow, spurring job creation, and strengthening the economy in 2011. Economists believe this could increase GDP by about 1% over the year to 3.9%.

> *Why did they extend the tax cuts? Because they want people to spend the money! If we squirrel it all away, it won't do us any good.*
>
> — Gary Keller

EXTENDED:
CONFORMING LOAN LIMITS

To increase the credit available in the higher-priced markets, the limits on conforming loans in the housing recovery bill first introduced in 2008 have been extended through September of 2011. This measure raises the limit in high-cost areas to a maximum of $729,750 from $417,000 everywhere. Without this measure, even standard homes in some markets would fall into the "jumbo loan" category. Financing will continue to be readily available to those buyers interested in that price range.

> *The extension of conforming loans is not a fix for affordability but it is a Band-Aid.*
>
> — Gary Keller

HALTED:
NEW MORTGAGE DISCLOSURE RULES

The Fed held off on finalizing pending rule changes under Regulation Z of the Truth in Lending Act (TILA) that would have mandated new consumer disclosure requirements for closed-end mortgage loans, home equity lines of credit, and reverse mortgages. The newly created Consumer Financial Protection Bureau will be required to combine the mortgage disclosures required by both TILA and RESPA in a single form. The rulemakings were initiated in response to claims that homeowners were signing up for unsustainable and unsuitable mortgages without understanding the terms of the loans during the boom years, which fueled unsound lending practices and led to the mortgage market meltdown in 2007.

Vision - Canada

Economic Snapshot - Canada 23
5 Canadian Statistics 24
    1. Home Sales Cool 24
    2. Home Prices Continue Upward Trend 25
    3. Inventory Stabilizes 26
    4. Mortgage Rates 27
    5. Affordability Improves Slightly 27
Events That Drive the Numbers - Canada 28
    1. Canada's Monetary Stimulus Continues
       to Boost the Market 28
    2. Implementation of New, Tighter Mortgage Rules 28
    3. Improving Credit Market 29
    4. Available Sides Per Agent 29
    5. Strong Currency 29
What the Canadian Government Is Doing 30
    Agreement Reached Between Competition Bureau
    and CREA 30
    Tightening Mortgage Regulations 30
Commercial Real Estate - Canada 31
    Vacancy Rates Remain Steady 31

Economic Snapshot - Canada

The economic health of Canada can be revealed through three markers: *gross domestic product (GDP)*, *inflation*, and *unemployment*.

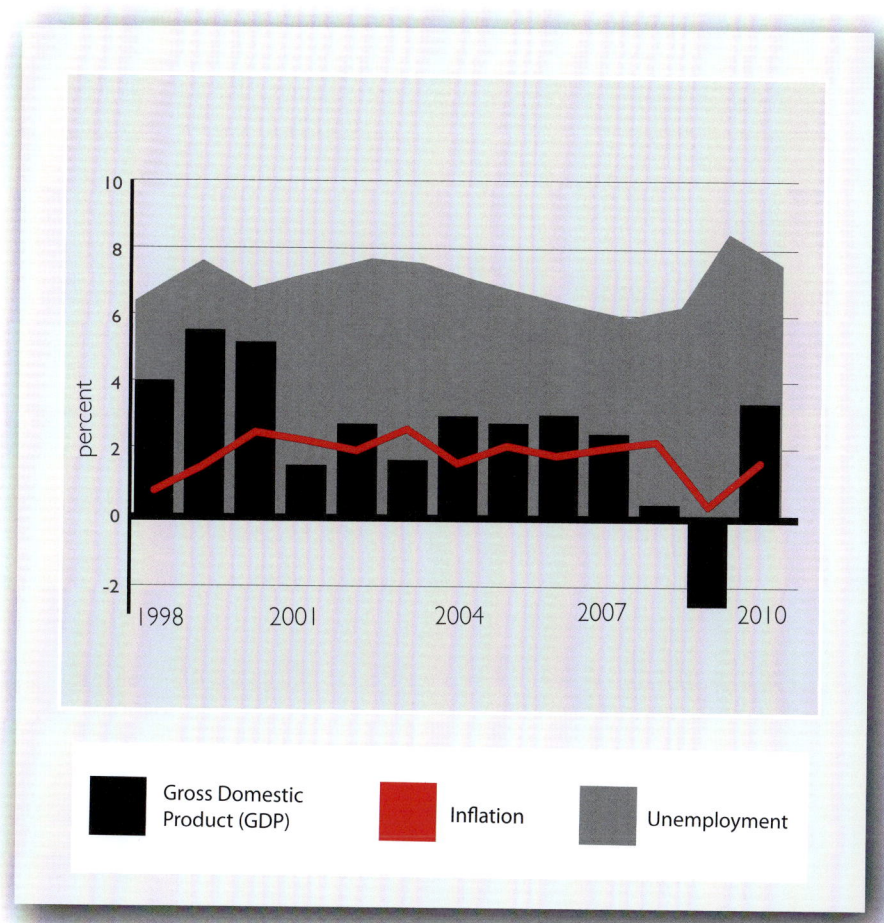

Inflation

The current target inflation rate is 2%, and inflation is expected to remain near that 2% target.

The hallmark of the Canadian economy is stability.

— Gary Keller

GDP

Supported by household and government spending, real GDP is close to its prerecession level, supported by household and government spending. When the final numbers are in, the Canadian economy is expected to have grown 3.5% in 2010 after having contracted by 2.5% in 2009. Stronger U.S. growth has brightened the outlook for Canadian exports, especially with the latest spurt in U.S. auto sales.

Unemployment

The rate stood at 7.6% in December 2010, down from 8.4% a year ago. While there were notable employment increases in December in manufacturing, transportation, and warehousing, there were declines in construction, health care and social assistance, trade, and business building.

KW MARKET NAVIGATOR 2011

5 Canadian Statistics

Every Agent Should Know

The housing market continues its relatively stable trend. Keep this information at your fingertips as you inform and advise your clients on what is happening in the market.

1 HOME SALES COOL

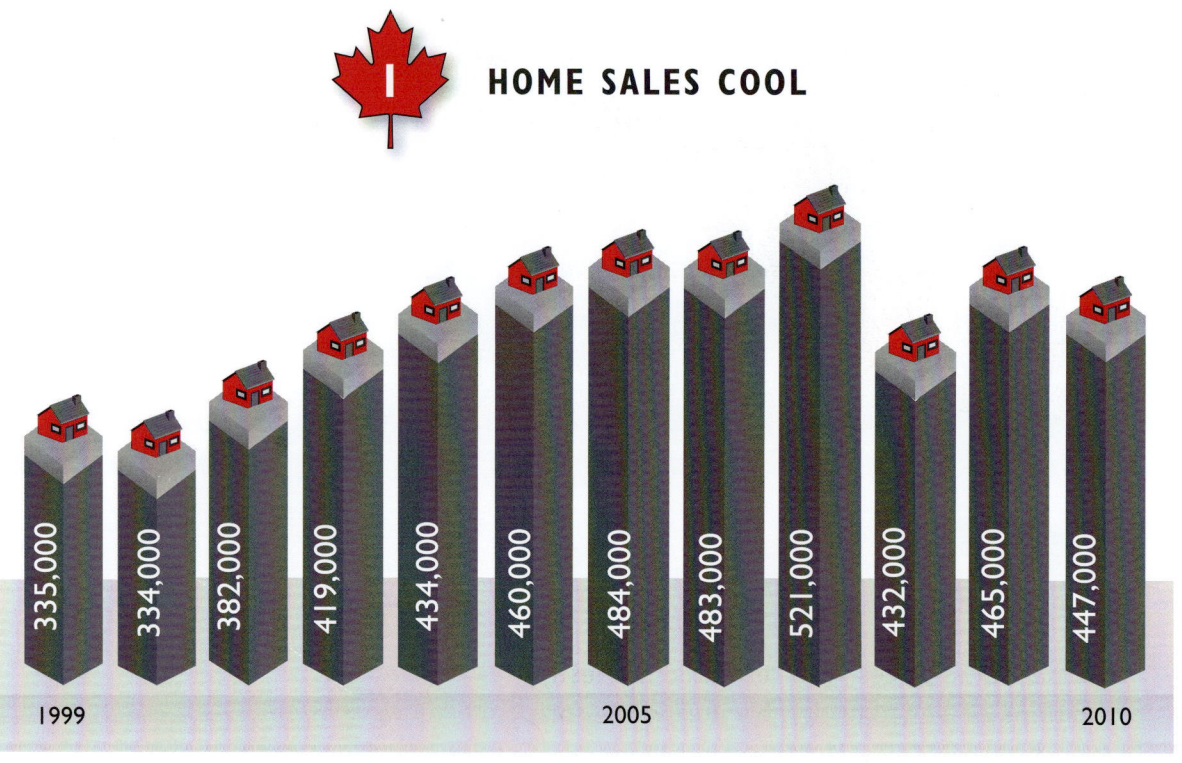

Sales activity has cooled, closing the year 3.9% below 2009.
2010 was still the sixth-highest annual activity level on record.

HOME PRICES CONTINUE UPWARD TREND

Appreciation Rates	
1980s	9.12%
1990s	1.20%
2000s	7.73%

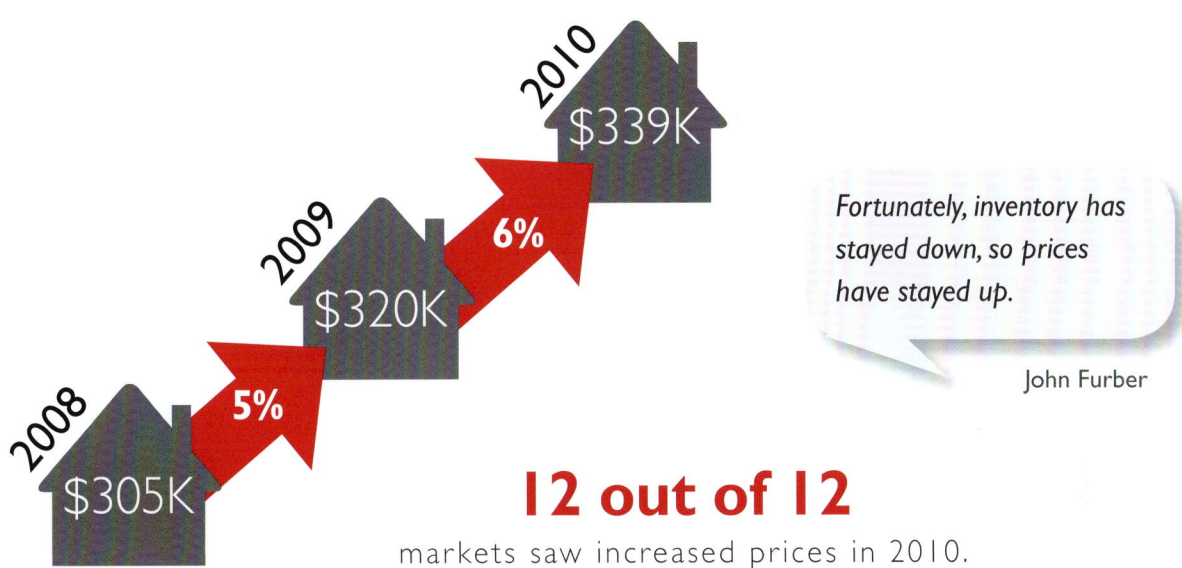

Fortunately, inventory has stayed down, so prices have stayed up.

John Furber

12 out of 12
markets saw increased prices in 2010.

National home prices have retreated modestly in recent months, as market conditions cooled considerably during the spring and summer of 2010 from their earlier boil. The softening of demand and a steady supply of homes available for sale in 2009 until early 2011 have brought the market into balance.

KW MARKET NAVIGATOR 2011

INVENTORY STABILIZES

The Canadian housing market remained balanced throughout 2010, as the supply side continued to adjust to the weaker demand and is likely to remain balanced going forward.

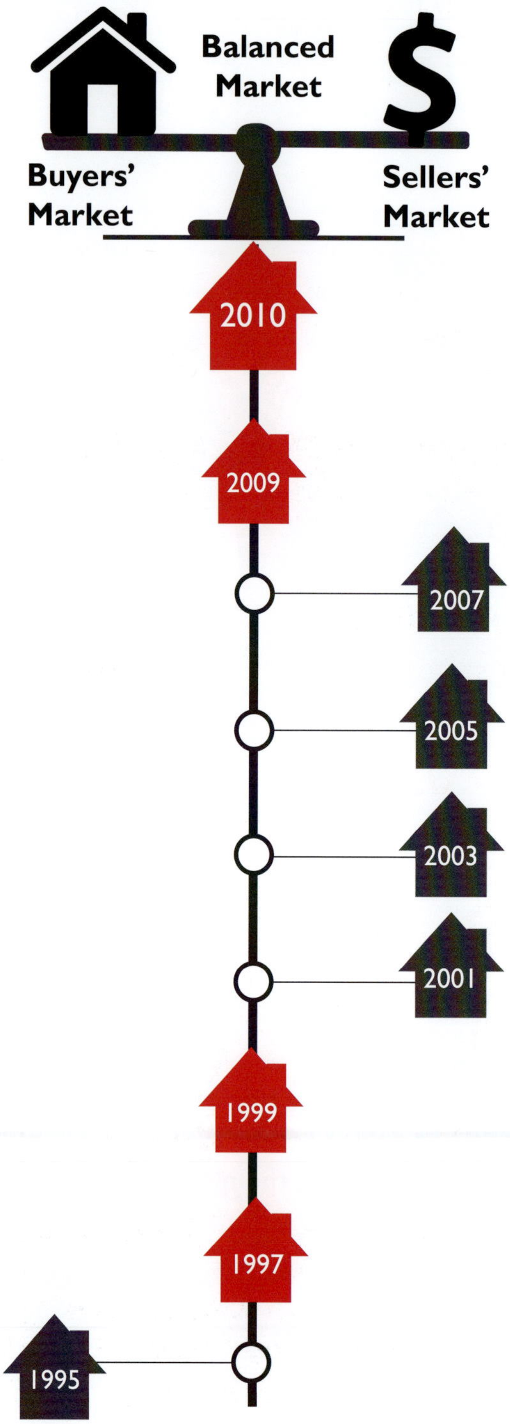

It's truly amazing that 1995 is the last time we had a buyers' market.

John Furber

4. MORTGAGE RATES

Now is the time to lock in a mortgage, as rates averaged 5.19% in December 2010, a drop of 0.3% from 5.49% in December 2009. The five-year fixed mortgage rates averaged 5.61% in 2010, the lowest on record dating back to 1973. They generally only have one direction to go—up.

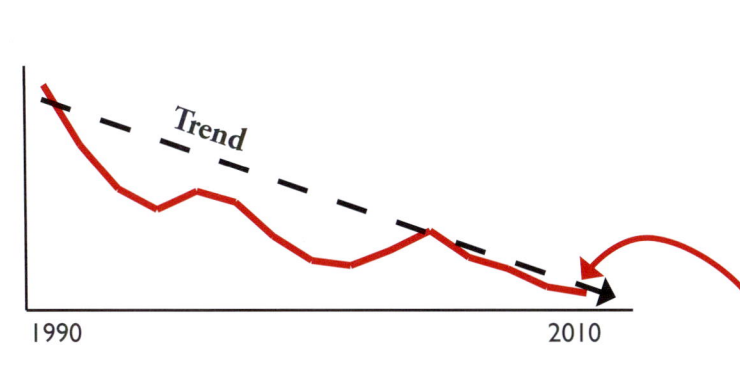

	1990	2010
Bread	$0.67	$2.22
Milk (L)	$0.59	$2.25
Gas (L)	$0.49	$1.01
House	$141,985	$339,030
*Monthly Payment	$1,554.24	$1,830.78
Mortgage Rate	**13.35%**	**5.61%**

*assuming 5-year fixed conventional mortgage with a 35-year mortization schedule.

---

5. AFFORDABILITY IMPROVES SLIGHTLY
Costs of Owning a Home in 2009 vs. 2010

0.23% more affordable than 2009

Two-Storey
0.3%
more affordable

Detached Bungalow
0.3%
more affordable

Condo
0.1%
more affordable

Affordability measures the amount of pretax income required to meet the costs of owning an averaged priced home: mortgage payments, utilities, and property taxes. All provinces saw improvements in affordability, and the biggest drop occurred in British Columbia.

Events That Drive the Numbers - Canada

The evolution of events in 2010 continued to shape the real estate market at the national level.

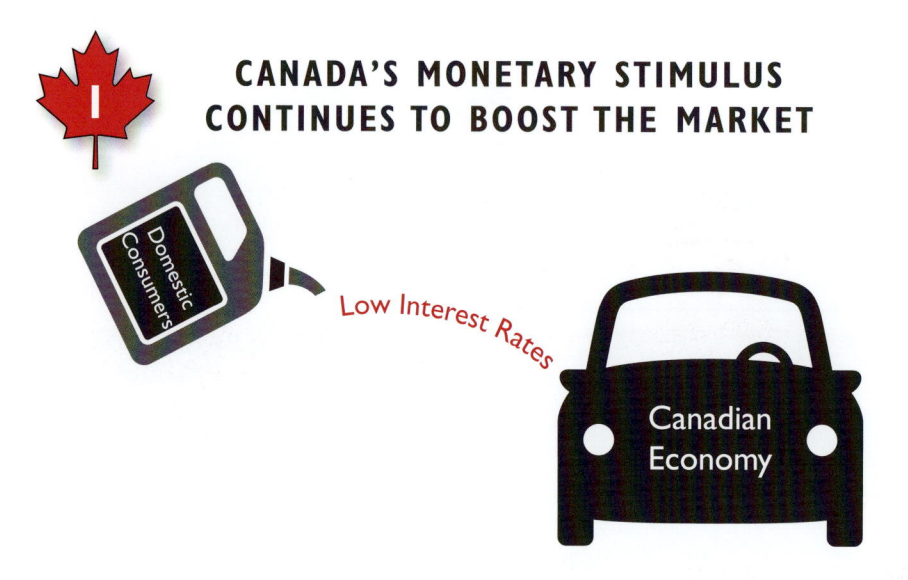

1. CANADA'S MONETARY STIMULUS CONTINUES TO BOOST THE MARKET

Considerable monetary stimulus in place has kept interest rates hovering around record-low levels. Domestic consumers have been able to fuel a lot of the recovery thanks to low interest rates that stimulated the financing and purchasing of property. This was an unexpected consequence, as consumer spending is a much smaller part of the economy than in the United States.

2. IMPLEMENTATION OF NEW, TIGHTER MORTGAGE RULES

Changes in mortgage rules created bumps in the market this year as buyers rushed to get in before the new rules came into effect. The new Harmonized Sales Tax increases the tax cost for new home sales and real estate commission but does not affect existing home sales/resales. The most notable change to the mortgage regulations is that the down payment to qualify for government-backed insurance is now 20% of the home price.

IMPROVING CREDIT MARKET

3 Spurred on by fear of the financial crisis in the United States, Canadian lending institutions tightened up their lending standards starting in 2008. During 2010, the government put several programs in place, which have since gained traction, to help open up more credit to consumers.

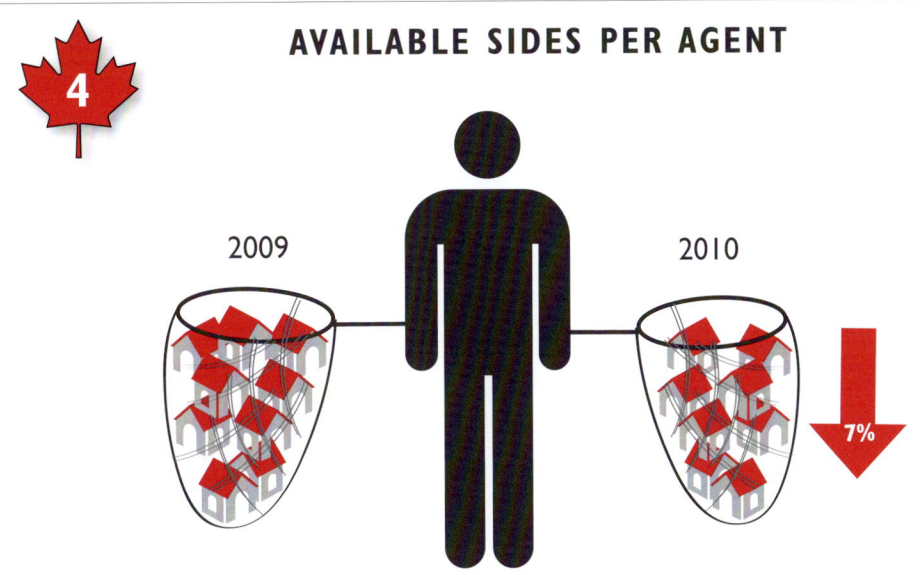

AVAILABLE SIDES PER AGENT

4

2009   2010

7%

Softer home sales and a steady rise in The Canadian Real Estate Association (CREA) membership pushed the number of sides available per agent down 7% from 9.5 in 2009 to 8.8 in 2010 from the previous year. It is still above the average over the past twenty years.

STRONG CURRENCY

5 Although Canada's currency is strong compared to most other advanced economies, it creates a competitive disadvantage for exports, which are a major component of the Canadian economy. A strong currency is also a testament to the strength of the countries economy and makes importing and traveling abroad more affordable for Canadians.

> *Our currency is the strongest it has been in years, and naturally we are excited about that. This is great for Canadians who want to invest in the Sunshine States.*

John Furber

What the Canadian Government Is Doing

The picture in Canada has improved across the board, coming into the recession well after the United States and being among the first to emerge. The government's proactive initiative to bolster the long-term stability of the financial, banking, and housing market is a positive sign of continued strength for Canada.

AGREEMENT REACHED BETWEEN COMPETITION BUREAU AND CREA

After more than three years of raging debate, in February 2010, delegates from Canada's 101 local real estate boards cast their votes for the settlement to resolve anticompetition charges with the Competition Bureau. The ratification inaugurated a ten-year, legally binding agreement through which CREA has agreed that its rules, as well as those of its members, should not deny or discriminate against agents—typically discount or fee-for-service agents—wishing to offer mere posting services. An important implication of this agreement is the possible accelerated creation of discount or other alternatives to the full-service brokerages.

TIGHTENING MORTGAGE REGULATIONS

After seeing the impact of unsound lending practices in the United States, over the past two years, Canada has reined in several measures, such as extending mortgages from 25 to 40 years, 100% financing, and 95% loan-to-value refinancing.

The key provisions are as follows:

- The maximum loan-to-value for refinancing will fall from 90% to 85%, meaning that homeowners will need to retain a greater amount of equity in the home when refinancing.

- The government will no longer support insurance on home equity lines of credit, also known as HELOCs.

- The maximum term (amortization period) for a government-backed insured mortgage will fall from 35 to 30 years.

The change in the maximum amortization period will likely impact the housing market the most. The shortened loan term will increase the monthly payments, even if the mortgage rates stay exactly the same, meaning that buyers will need to have 5% to 8% higher incomes to qualify for the same priced homes. Additionally, as first-time buyers must now take out mortgages with shorter terms, this measure may delay their entry into the market.

Commercial Real Estate - Canada

Commercial real estate has not been overbuilt and no major developers have gone bankrupt. Slow and stable growth in new development is expected to continue. In the industrial sector, new development is tempered by slow growth in the U.S. economy.

VACANCY RATES REMAIN STEADY
2010

Office
9% Vacancy

Industrial
7% Vacancy

Multifamily
3% Vacancy

Healthy vacancy rates in the office sector are less than half the rates in the United States, and office properties offer reliable cash flow opportunities to investors. Only marginal improvements can be expected in industrial rent and vacancy until exports, specifically exports to the United States, improve. There is high demand for multifamily apartment buildings and few opportunities to purchase. Immigration and relatively high home prices in some areas keep tenant demand strong.

OFFICE VACANCIES

1999 — 2010

Vision – Perspective and Action

3

How Do We Recover?..35
The 4 Gears of Success 36–37

How Do We Recover?

Four Stages

Every market in every economy goes through four stages of recovery. This is the blueprint on how to run a government and keep the housing economy moving.

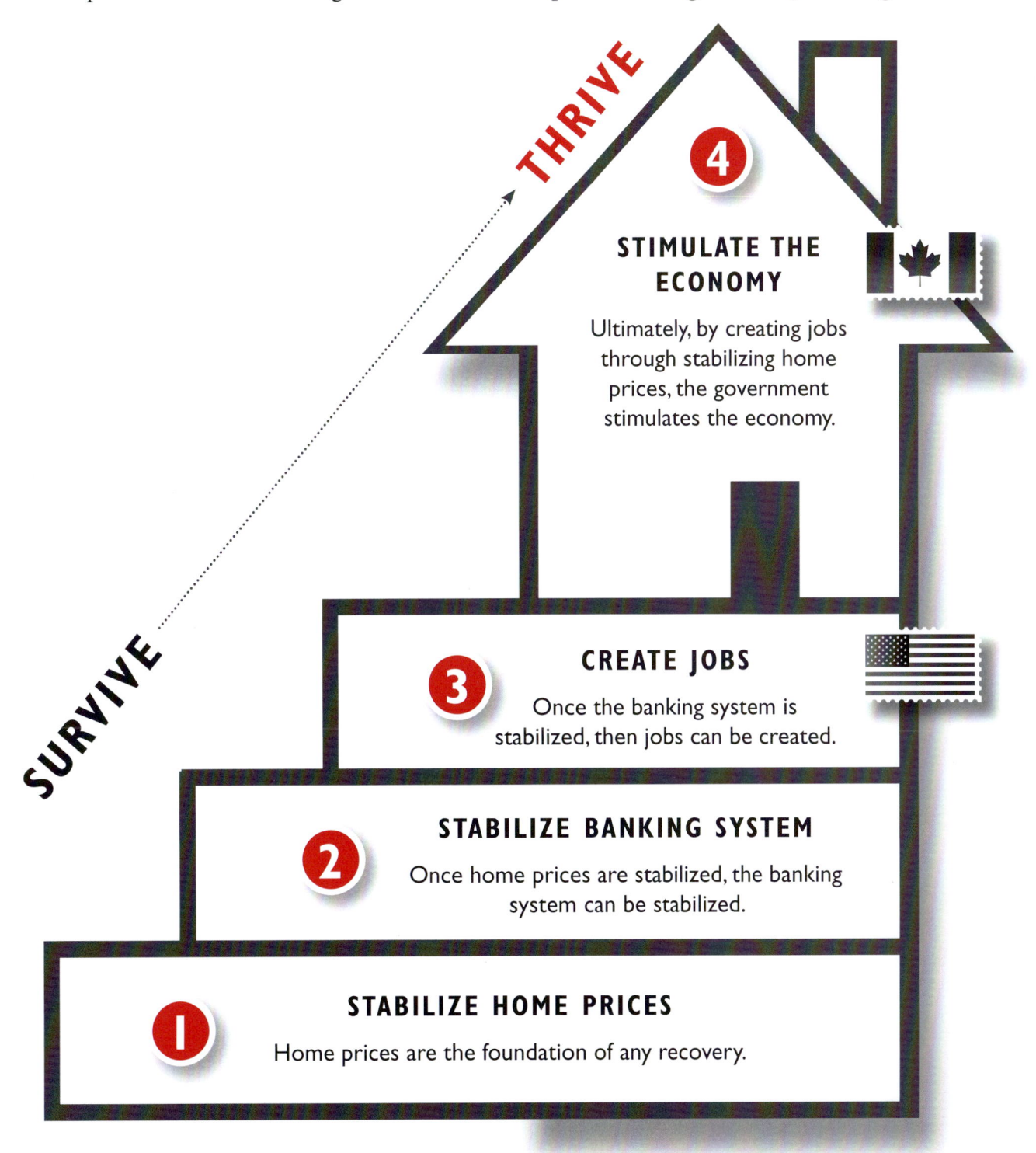

THRIVE

4 STIMULATE THE ECONOMY
Ultimately, by creating jobs through stabilizing home prices, the government stimulates the economy.

SURVIVE

3 CREATE JOBS
Once the banking system is stabilized, then jobs can be created.

2 STABILIZE BANKING SYSTEM
Once home prices are stabilized, the banking system can be stabilized.

1 STABILIZE HOME PRICES
Home prices are the foundation of any recovery.

The 4 Gears

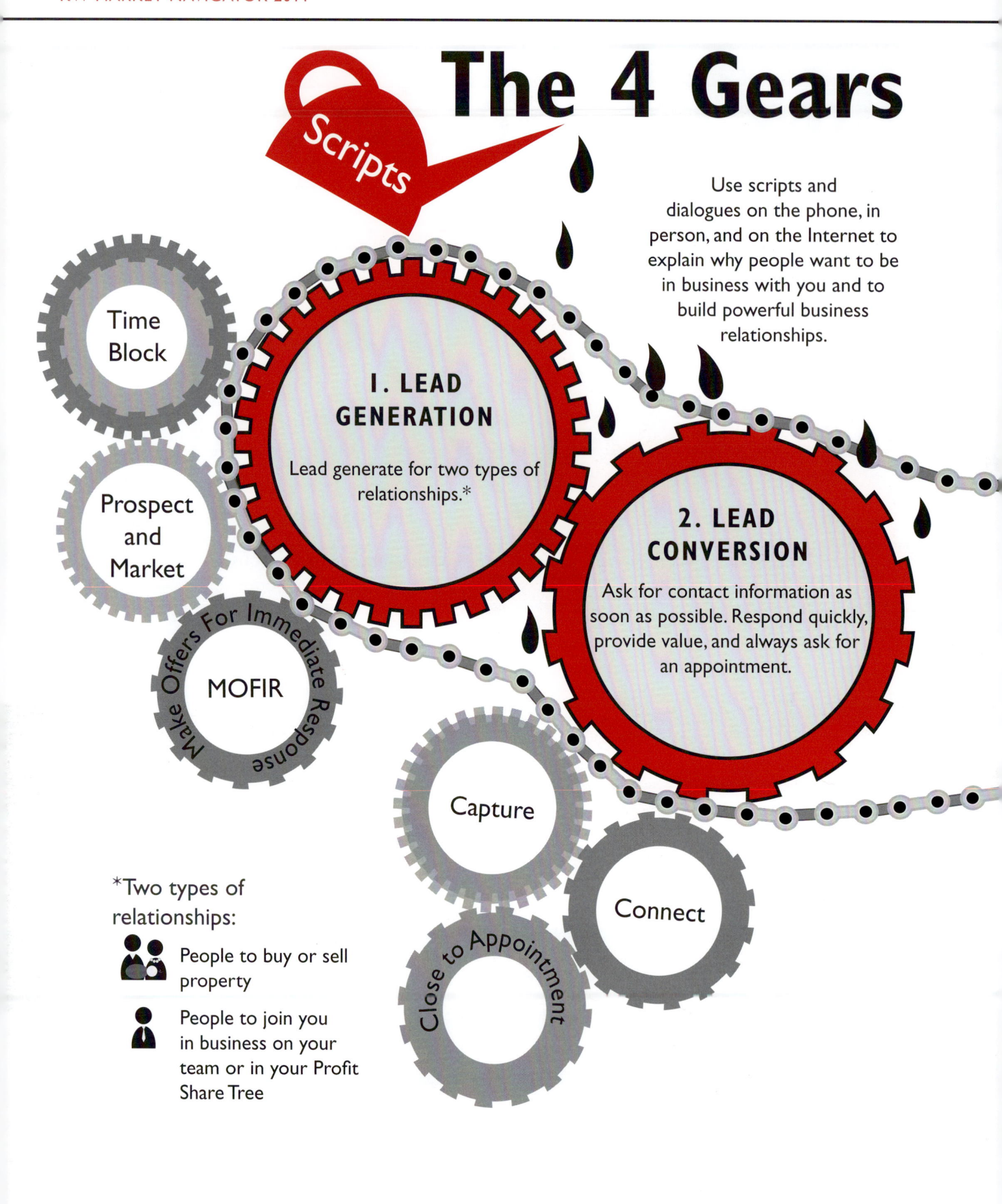

Scripts

Use scripts and dialogues on the phone, in person, and on the Internet to explain why people want to be in business with you and to build powerful business relationships.

- Time Block
- Prospect and Market
- MOFIR (Make Offers For Immediate Response)

1. LEAD GENERATION

Lead generate for two types of relationships.*

2. LEAD CONVERSION

Ask for contact information as soon as possible. Respond quickly, provide value, and always ask for an appointment.

- Capture
- Close to Appointment
- Connect

*Two types of relationships:
- People to buy or sell property
- People to join you in business on your team or in your Profit Share Tree

# of Success

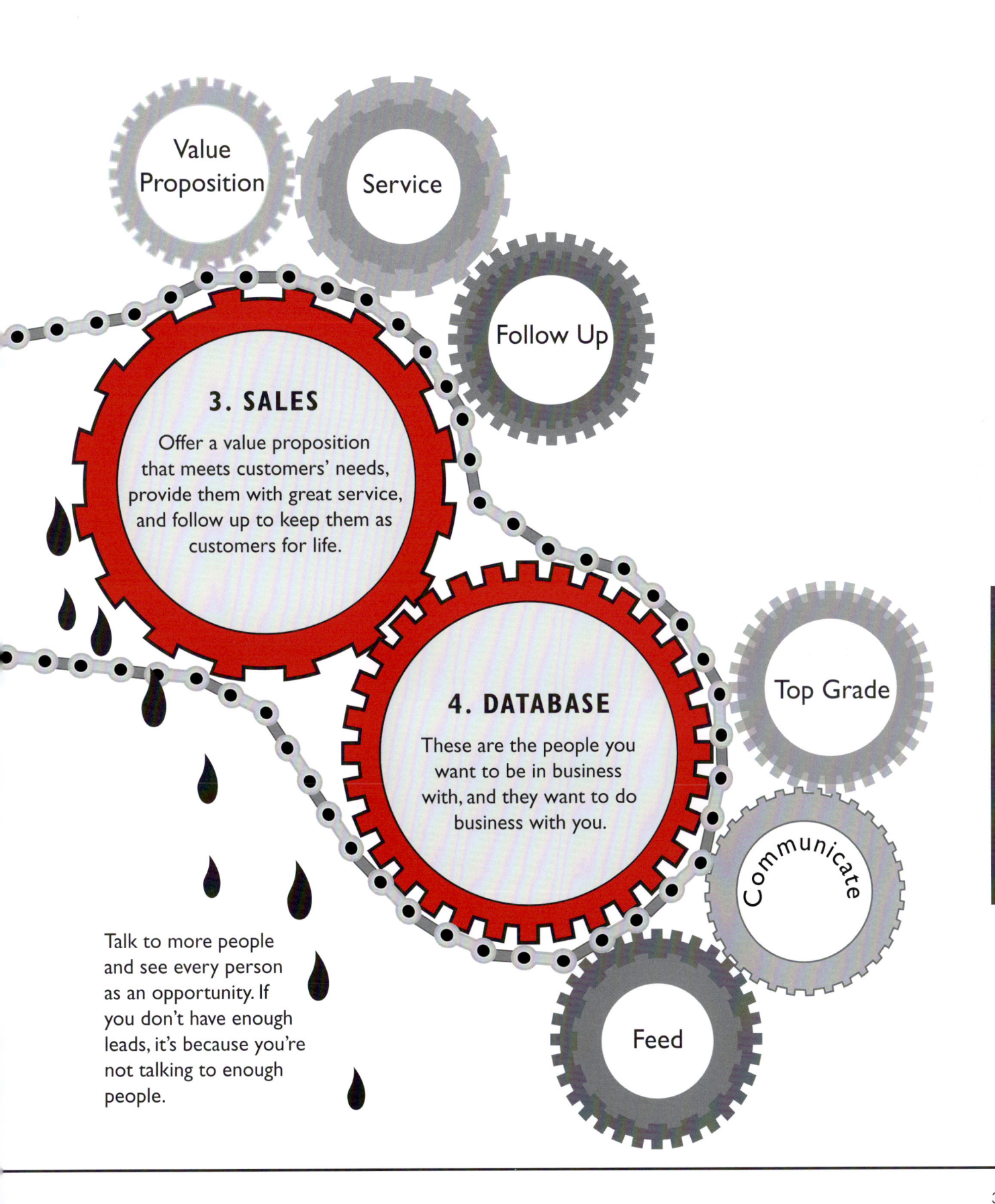

Value Proposition

Service

Follow Up

3. SALES
Offer a value proposition that meets customers' needs, provide them with great service, and follow up to keep them as customers for life.

4. DATABASE
These are the people you want to be in business with, and they want to do business with you.

Top Grade

Communicate

Feed

Talk to more people and see every person as an opportunity. If you don't have enough leads, it's because you're not talking to enough people.

Sharpen Your Focus

Keller Williams Research

Home Buyers

MORTGAGE RATES REACH RECORD LOWS 42

HOME PRICES STABILIZE 43

AFFORDABILITY AT RECORD LEVELS 43

HOME BUYERS' RELATIONSHIP STATUS 44

AVERAGE AGE OF HOME BUYERS................................. 44

TYPE OF HOME PURCHASED.. 45

PRICE IS THE MOST IMPORTANT FACTOR
FOR BUYERS 46

WHY BUYERS BUY... 46

LOCATION PREFERENCES.. 47

LENGTH OF BUYER CONSULTATION 48

BUYER CONSULTATION 49

TIME-SAVING TIPS 49

TAX CREDIT 50

BUYER QUALIFICATION... 50

GOING GREEN: TOP FIVE GREEN FEATURES 51

INTEREST IN GREEN FEATURES................................... 51

Now's the Time to Buy

It's always a great time to buy a fantastic piece of real estate. Today that's truer than ever. The affordability of homes is lower than it's been in a generation, and mortgages hit a historic low in 2010. Foreclosures and short sales continue to represent more than one-third of the market, and are often 30% below market value. This golden age of buying is showing some signs that it won't last forever; prices have essentially stabilized and inventory is steadily shrinking in most markets. Encourage your buyers to strike now so they can look back and say, "I'm glad I did," rather than "I wish I had."

> *If you don't own a home, buy one; if you own one home, buy another; and if you own two homes, buy a third and lend your relatives the money to buy a home. Your debt and interest payments get locked in at record lows, while the price of your home is still safe.*
>
> John Paulson
> Multibillionaire Hedge Fund Operator,
> Forbes.com

MORTGAGE RATES REACH RECORD LOWS

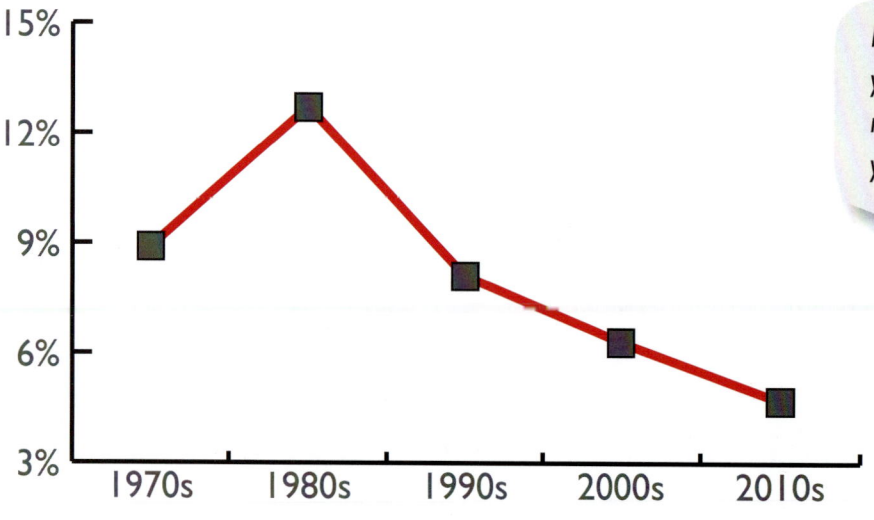

> *If inflation picks up, you won't see these mortgage rates again in your lifetime.*
>
> Brett Arends
> *The Wall Street Journal*
> September 16, 2010

KW RESEARCH

HOME PRICES STABILIZE

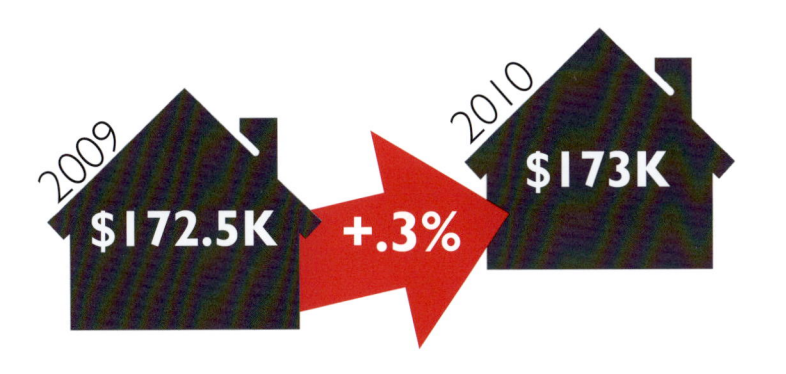

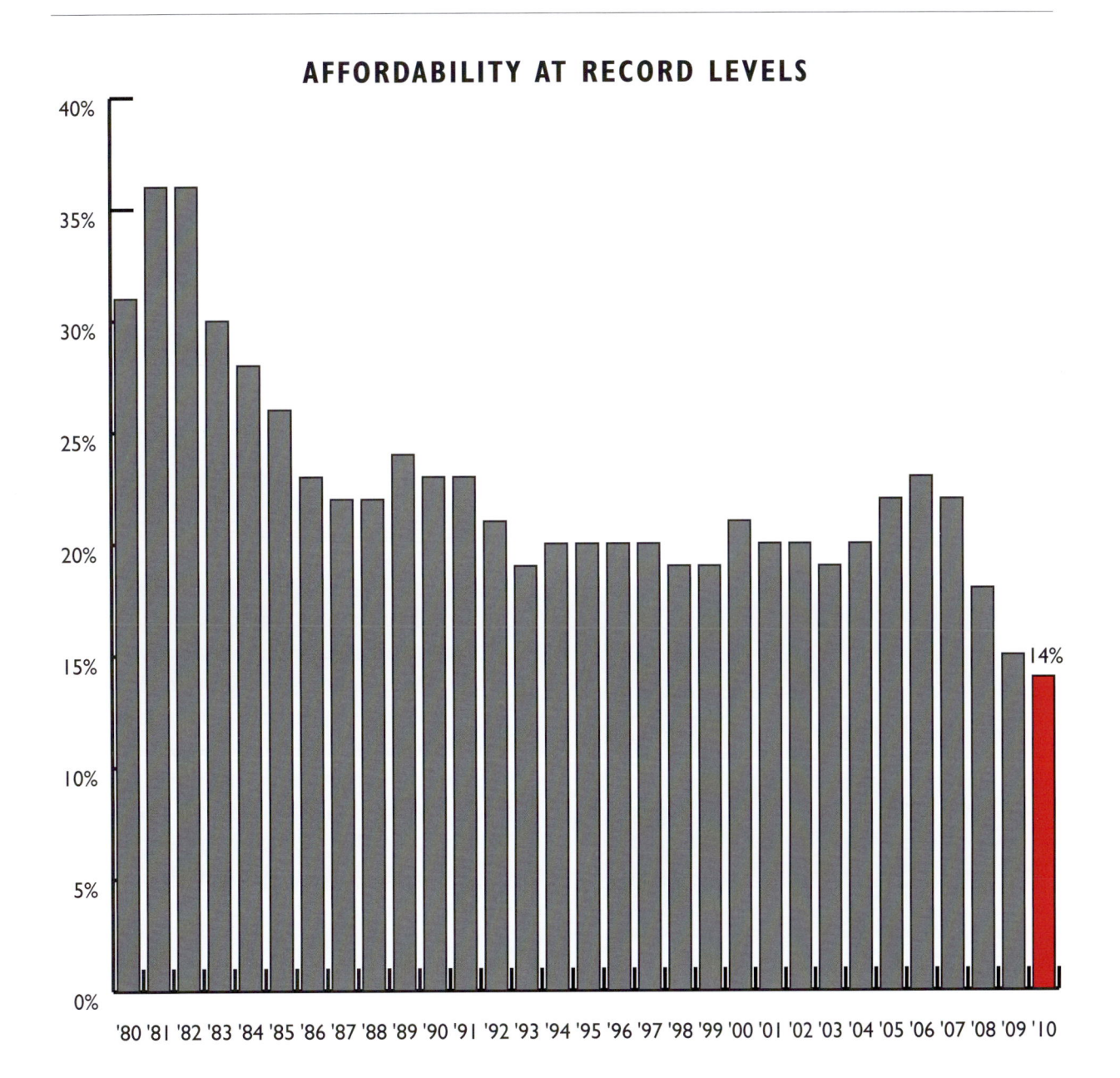

2009 $172.5K +.3% → 2010 $173K

AFFORDABILITY AT RECORD LEVELS

'80 '81 '82 '83 '84 '85 '86 '87 '88 '89 '90 '91 '92 '93 '94 '95 '96 '97 '98 '99 '00 '01 '02 '03 '04 '05 '06 '07 '08 '09 '10 — 14%

4. HOME BUYERS

43

HOME BUYERS' RELATIONSHIP STATUS

65% of all buyers are couples

34% of all buyers are single

1% are multiple buyers

WHAT THIS MEANS FOR YOU:

Knowing who is buying will help you fine-tune your marketing and prospecting messages. Consider purchasing data sets of consumers who comprise your target markets.

AVERAGE AGE OF HOME BUYERS

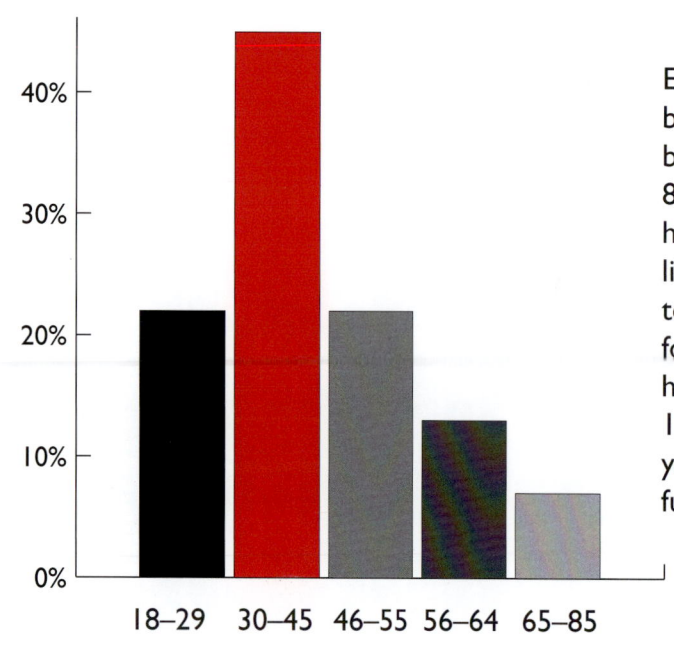

AGE: 18–29, 30–45, 46–55, 56–64, 65–85

Echo boomers—children of the baby boomers—are the generation born between 1979–1995. Approximately 80 million strong, they are entering the housing market and fueling growth just like the boomers before them, according to Harvard University's Joint Center for Housing Studies. The report states household growth should range between 12.5 to 14.8 million over the next ten years, creating a powerful driver of future demand and growth.

TYPE OF HOME PURCHASED

82%
Single-Family Detached

9%
Condominium

7%
Town House

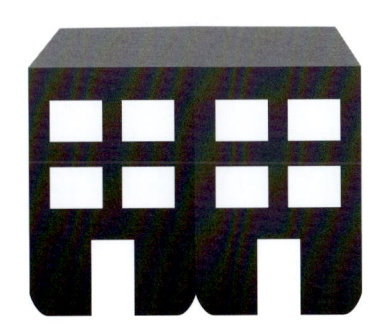

1%
Duplex

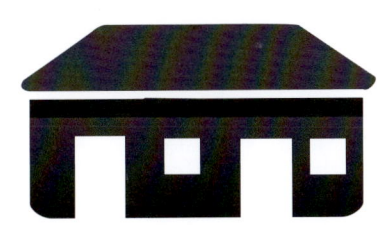

PRICE IS THE MOST IMPORTANT FACTOR FOR BUYERS

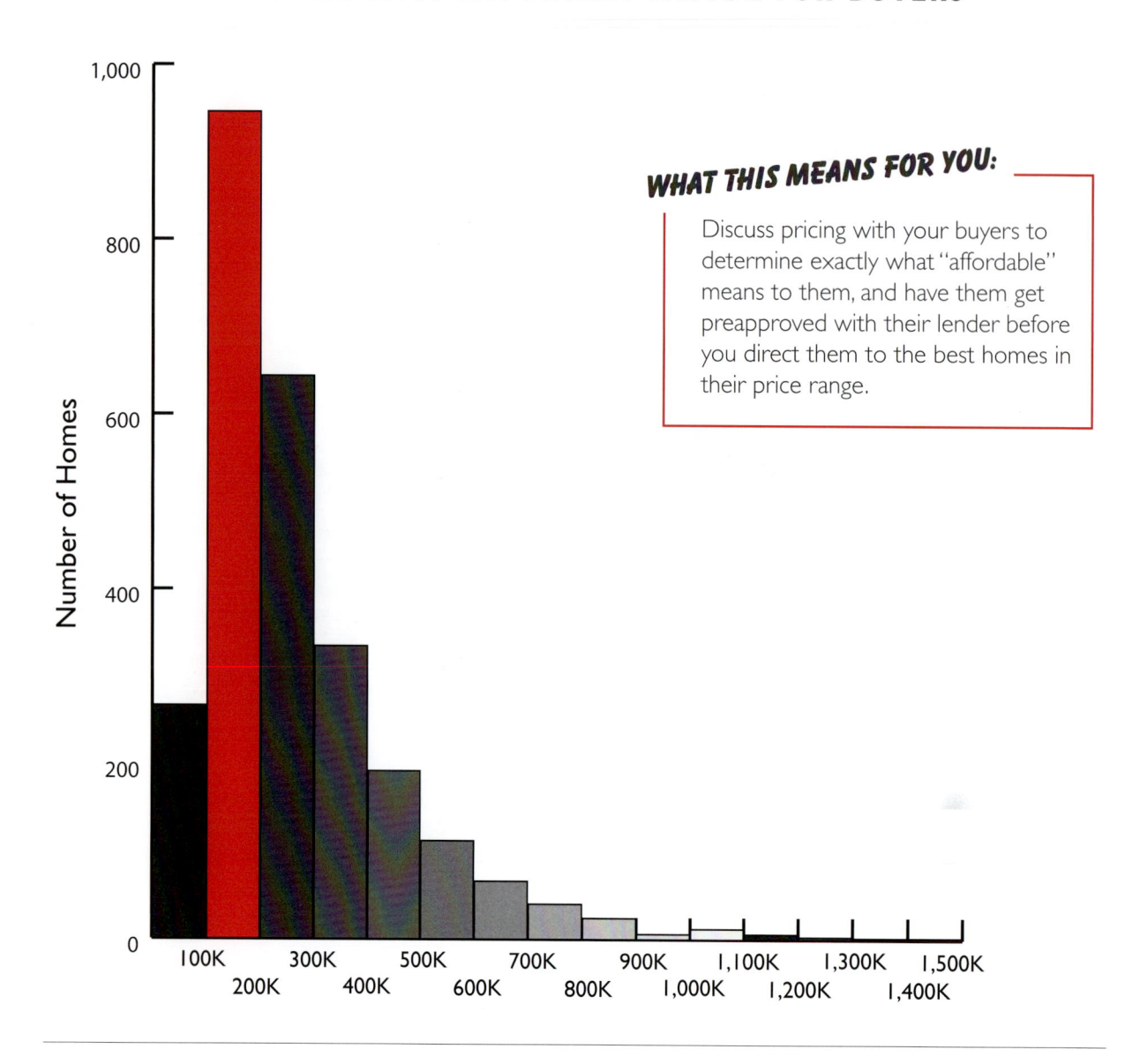

Number of Homes (y-axis: 0 to 1,000) by price (x-axis: 100K to 1,500K)

WHAT THIS MEANS FOR YOU:

Discuss pricing with your buyers to determine exactly what "affordable" means to them, and have them get preapproved with their lender before you direct them to the best homes in their price range.

WHY BUYERS BUY

- **Affordable Price** — 43%
- **Low Mortgage Rates** — 36%
- **Able to Afford** — 28%
- **Tired of Paying Rent** — 21%

LOCATION PREFERENCES

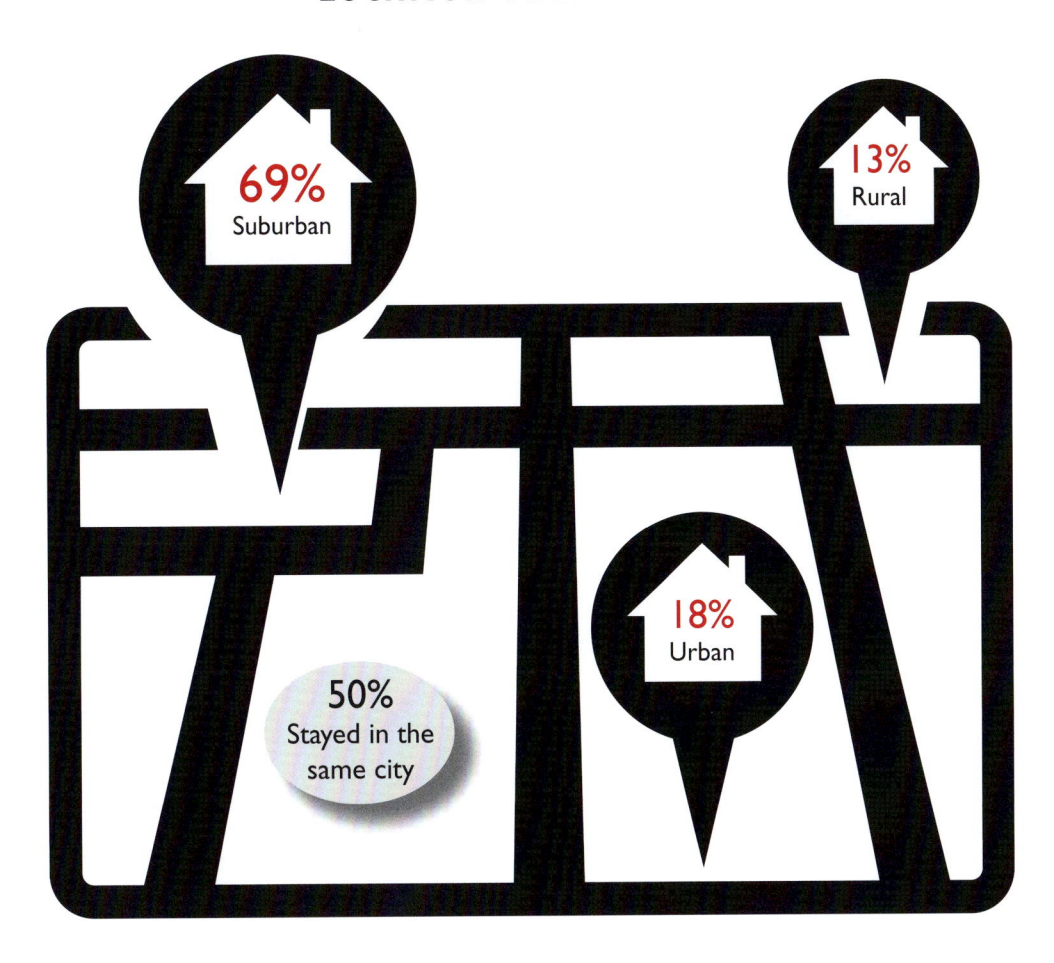

69% Suburban

13% Rural

18% Urban

50% Stayed in the same city

How Long Do Buyers Look?		
	Weeks	No. of Homes
Urban	6	11
Suburban	7	12
Rural	7	10
Different City	8	13
Same City	7	10

Why are people taking so long to purchase a home? They are not getting any better deals, they are just taking longer because they are in the driver's seat—they have lots of options and no pressure.

Gary Keller

LENGTH OF BUYER CONSULTATION

Excessively long consultations don't appear to be doing anyone any good. There are two apparent sweet spots, depending on skill and client needs: 15 or 90 minutes.

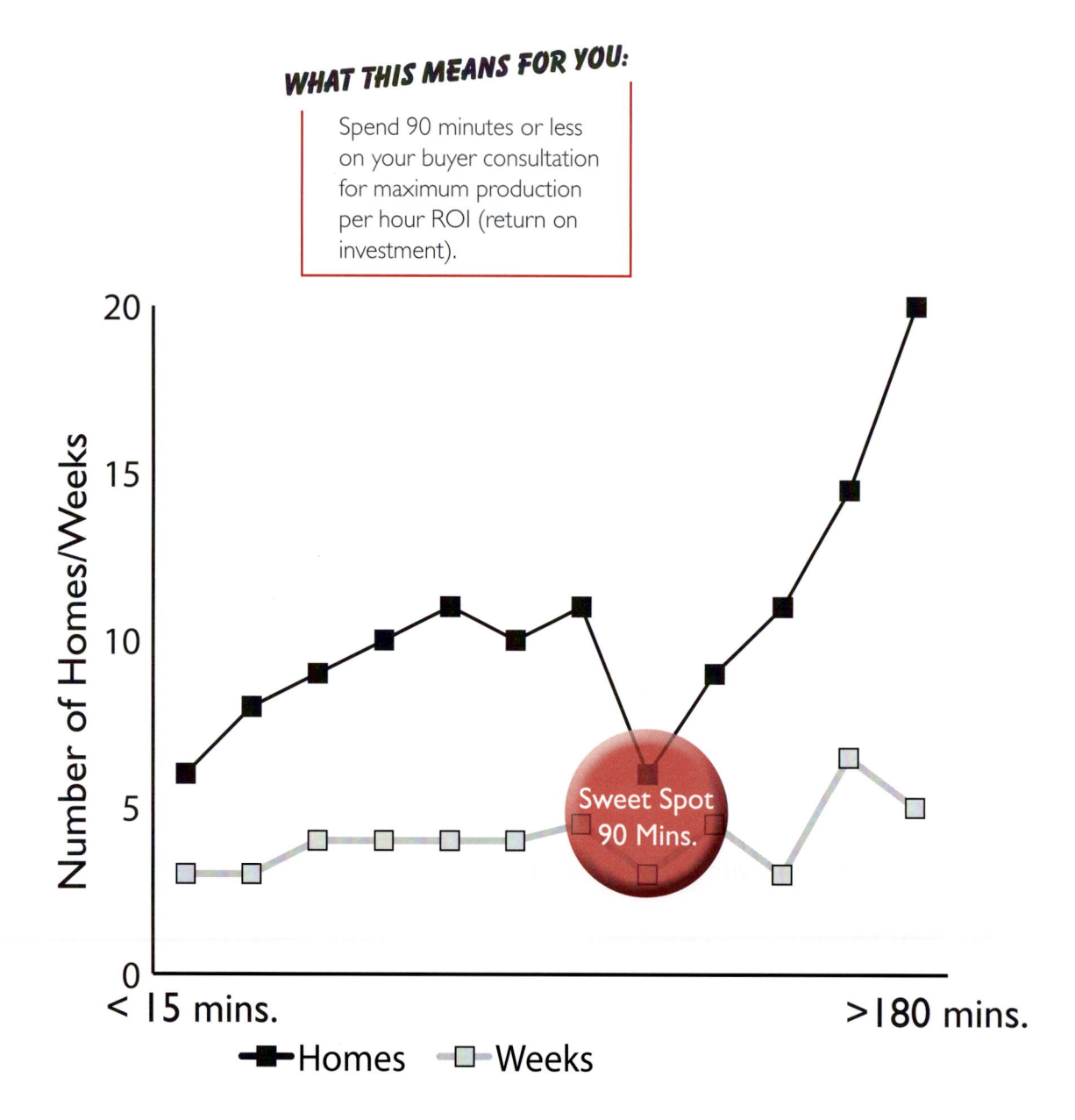

WHAT THIS MEANS FOR YOU:

Spend 90 minutes or less on your buyer consultation for maximum production per hour ROI (return on investment).

Sweet Spot 90 Mins.

─■─ Homes   ─□─ Weeks

BUYER CONSULTATION

91% Conducted a buyer consultation before showing the buyer the first house.

WHAT THIS MEANS FOR YOU:
The consultation is your time to educate your buyers, set expectations, and ask for the signed Buyer Representation Agreement.

YES

☐	Buyer Consultation	91%
☐	Discuss Buyers' Wants and Needs	91%
☐	Discuss Process of Buying	71%
☐	Sign an Exclusivity Agreement	50%

TIME-SAVING TIPS

Spending time in your car with buyers is not the most dollar-productive use of your time!

- Send buyers on a drive-by before you set a showing appointment.
- Periodically revisit your buyers' wants and needs to make sure you are still on the same page.
- Use this script: "My job is not to show you every house on the market. My job is to find and show you the right house."

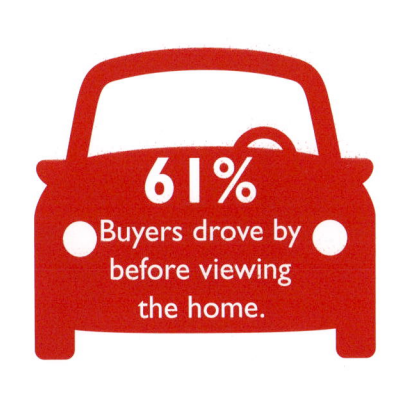

61% Buyers drove by before viewing the home.

Number of Offers Buyers Made	
Type of Market	Offers
Buyers'	2
Balanced	2
Sellers'	3

TAX CREDIT

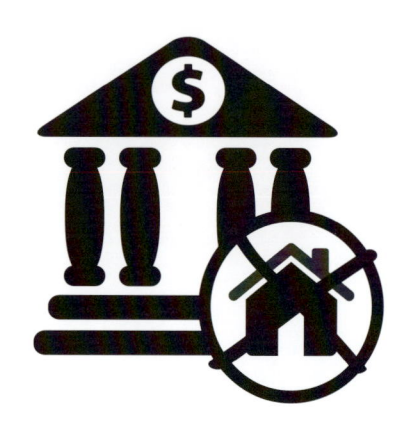

72% of buyers were still interested in buying after the tax credit expired.

BUYER QUALIFICATION

41% Buyers Prequalified

64% Buyers Preapproved

GOING GREEN: TOP FIVE GREEN FEATURES

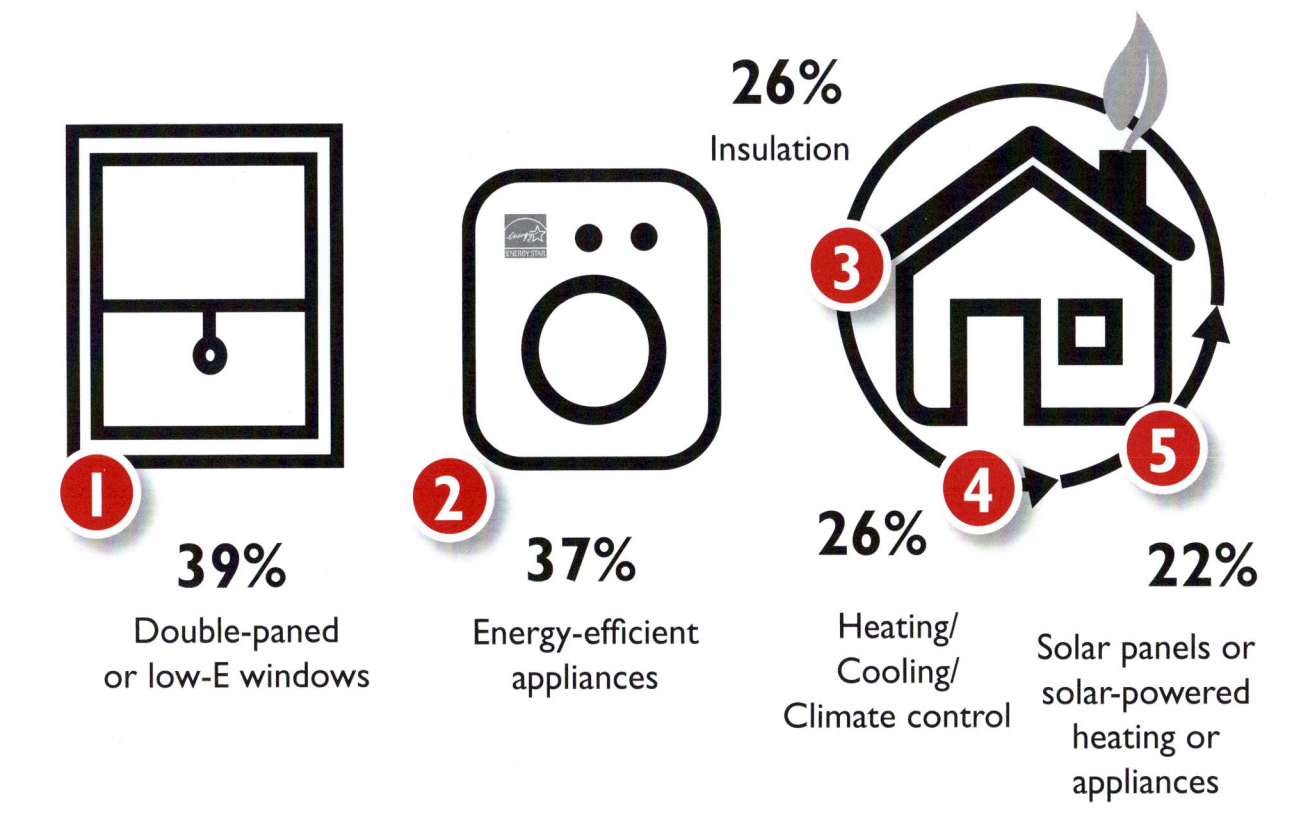

1. 39% — Double-paned or low-E windows

2. 37% — Energy-efficient appliances

3. 26% — Insulation

4. 26% — Heating/Cooling/Climate control

5. 22% — Solar panels or solar-powered heating or appliances

INTEREST IN GREEN FEATURES

- **89%** Families with Children
- **54%** Singles

4. HOME BUYERS

First-Time Home Buyers

- Marital Status of First-Time Home Buyers 54
- Family Makeup of First-Time Home Buyers 55
- Generation X and Y 55
- Preferences Among First-Time Buyers 56
- Average Beds/Baths 56
- Interest in Nontraditional Transactions 57
- Home-Buying Criteria 58
- Key Triggers 59
- Key Activities Prior to Home Tours 60
- Percentage of Agents Who Do a Consultation with Their First-Time Home Buyers 61
- Most First-Time Home Buyer Consultations Lasted 30 Mins.–1 Hr. 61
- Most First-Time Home Buyers Had an Accepted Offer Within Three Days of Submission 61

First-Time Home Buyers

First-time home buyers represent a significant portion of the market—according to NAR statistics, it's a whopping 50%! Is your business set up and positioned to promote to this market segment? Working with first-time home buyers is rewarding and meaningful: You play an integral role in making dreams come true, and by encouraging them to make the leap to homeownership, you can get them started on a path of wealth building they may never even have considered before. While it may possibly be the most expensive investment they have ever made, it will also be one of the smartest.

MARITAL STATUS OF FIRST-TIME HOME BUYERS

57% of all first-time home buyers are couples

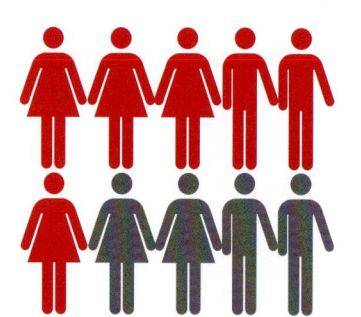

43% of all first-time home buyers are single

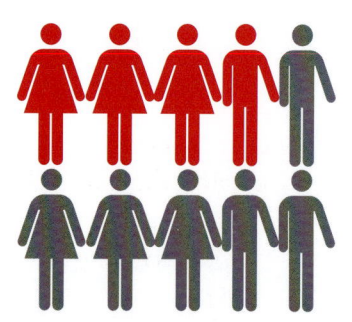

There are more single buyers out there than ever before. Could this be a result of the shrinking institution of marriage? According to a study from the Pew Research Center in 1960, 72% of American adults were married. By 2008, that share had fallen to 52%. This long-term trend may be solidifying: the Population Reference Bureau in Washington states more young couples are delaying marriage or forgoing it altogether—most likely a result of the economic downturn.

FAMILY MAKEUP OF FIRST-TIME HOME BUYERS

31% of all first-time home buyers are couples with children

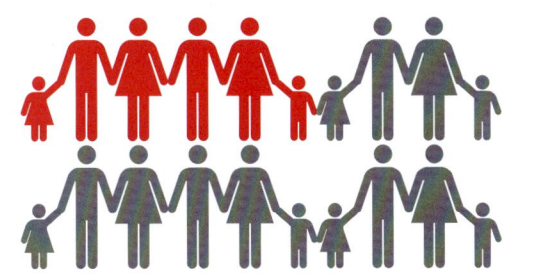

24% of all first-time home buyers are single with children

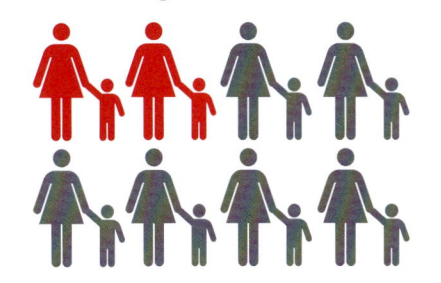

GENERATION X AND Y

Younger people are the highest percentage of first-time home buyers.

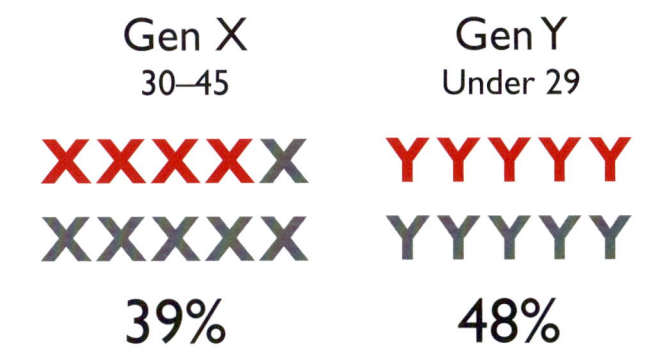

Gen X	Gen Y
30–45	Under 29
XXXXX	YYYYY
XXXXX	YYYYY
39%	48%

X – Largely born between 1965 and 1978. On the whole, they are more diverse in race, class, religion, and ethnicity than the baby boomers. The U.S. Census Bureau cites Generation X as statistically holding the highest education levels when looking at age group—more than 60% of Generation Xers attended college.

Y – Also known as "echo boomers" due to the significant increase in birth rates through the 1980s and into the 1990s, their numbers are estimated as high as 70 million. Generation Y is the fastest-growing segment of today's workforce. Armed with smartphones, laptops, and other technology, Generation Y is plugged in 24 hours a day, 7 days a week.

Characteristics of each generation vary by region, depending on social and economic conditions.

KW MARKET NAVIGATOR 2011

PREFERENCES AMONG FIRST-TIME BUYERS

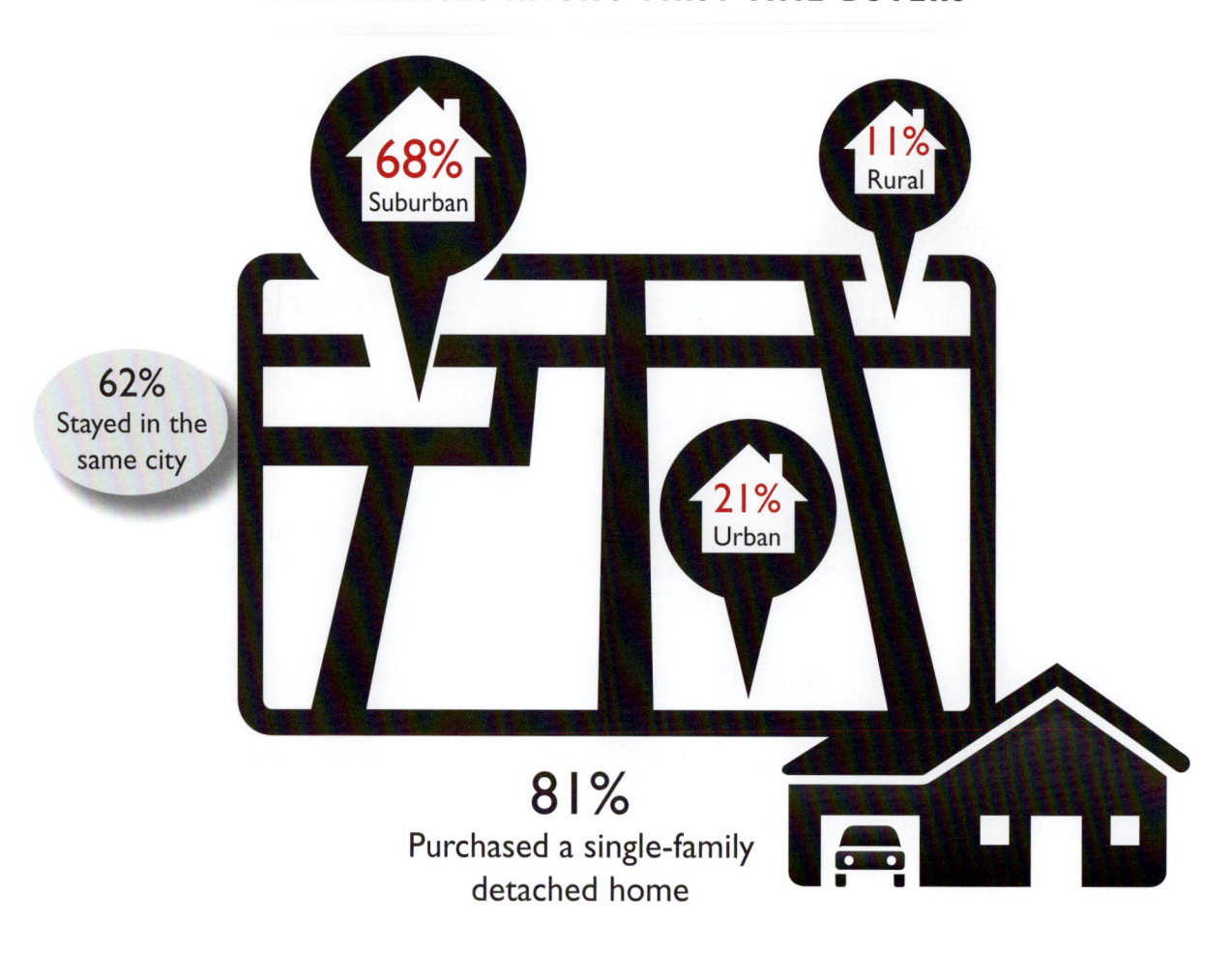

68% Suburban

11% Rural

21% Urban

62% Stayed in the same city

81% Purchased a single-family detached home

AVERAGE BEDS/BATHS

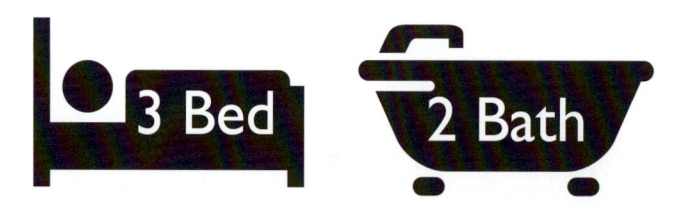

3 Bed   2 Bath

If you want your first-time home buyers to become clients for life, start by positioning yourself as their agent for life by encouraging them to keep their first sale in mind as they are making their first purchase. Use this information to show them what other first-time buyers are looking for, so they can purchase a home that will be a fast and profitable sale when they are ready to move on.

INTEREST IN NONTRADITIONAL TRANSACTIONS

29%
purchased a distressed property

16% purchased a foreclosure

13% purchased a short sale

Given that affordable pricing tops the list of motivation and criteria for buying, it's no surprise that many first-time home buyers purchase distressed properties, which can be up to 30% below market value. Be sure to show distressed properties to your cost-conscious buyers, while at the same time advising them of the potential hidden expenses—distressed properties can often entail a lot of work if they have been damaged or neglected in the process. Your buyers may prefer to buy a nondistressed property if, in the long run, it will cost the same but take much less time and effort. Another consideration is transaction time: short sales and REOs typically take considerably longer to close because you are dealing with institutions rather than individual sellers.

Distressed Property Price For First-Time Home Buyers	
Average	$185,971
Median	$153,000

Purchase Parameters

First-time home buyers may have an especially difficult time defining exactly what it is they are looking for in a home. The buyer consultation is the best time to define, refine, then maybe even redefine exactly what your first-time home buyers are looking for. These statistics can help them get started.

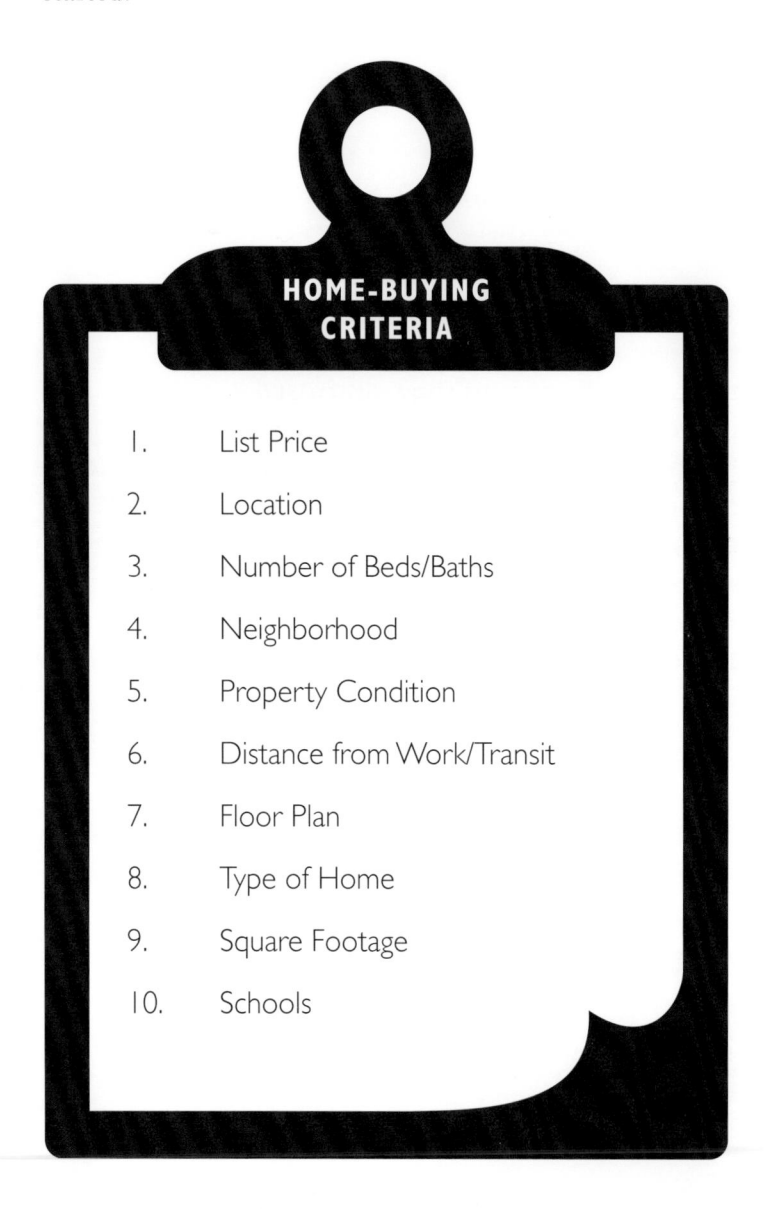

HOME-BUYING CRITERIA

1. List Price
2. Location
3. Number of Beds/Baths
4. Neighborhood
5. Property Condition
6. Distance from Work/Transit
7. Floor Plan
8. Type of Home
9. Square Footage
10. Schools

"You may think that shopping for homes starts with jumping in the car and driving all over town. And it's true that 'hopping in the car to look' is probably the most exciting part of the home-buying process. All those properties! All those neighborhoods! All those choices! However, driving around is fun for only so long—if weeks go by without finding what you're looking for, the fun can fade pretty fast. That's why we say that looking for homes begins with carefully assessing your values, wants, and needs, both for the short and for the long term.

"In short, we think your consultation session starts with your values. From there, you can explore your wants and needs. Once you understand that, you're ready to go back to the 'what': your final list of criteria."

Extract from chapter 4 of Your First Home.

Motivating Factors

Home buyers buy because they want to put down roots, have enough space for their family—and because it makes good financial sense. Five out of eight of the motivations for buying are related to money. Act as a fiduciary consultant with your buyers and guide them toward homes that will not only suit their immediate needs but will also provide the basis for wealth building.

"Many people don't come to realize the importance of financial independence until later in their lives when they are faced with a personal or family circumstance that requires available money—a health situation, college tuition, the loss of a job, a needed purchase, or retirement. For many of these same people, they are relieved and grateful that they had purchased a home and built some financial wealth to draw on. They realized, in fact, that their home was the best investment they had ever made. And, it saved the day. Homeownership becomes an 'intentional investment' that lays the foundation for a life of financial security, personal choice, and the ability to pay for whatever you need or want to pay for."

Extract from chapter 4 of Your First Home.

KEY TRIGGERS

1. Affordable Price
2. Mortgage Rate
3. Tired of Renting
4. Home Buyer Tax Credit
5. Steady Job
6. Equity
7. Family Situation Changed
8. Space

Your First Home is an easy, effective, and educational tool. Give it to all first-time home buyers and prospects.

www.facebook.com/YourFirstHome

KEY ACTIVITIES PRIOR TO HOME TOURS

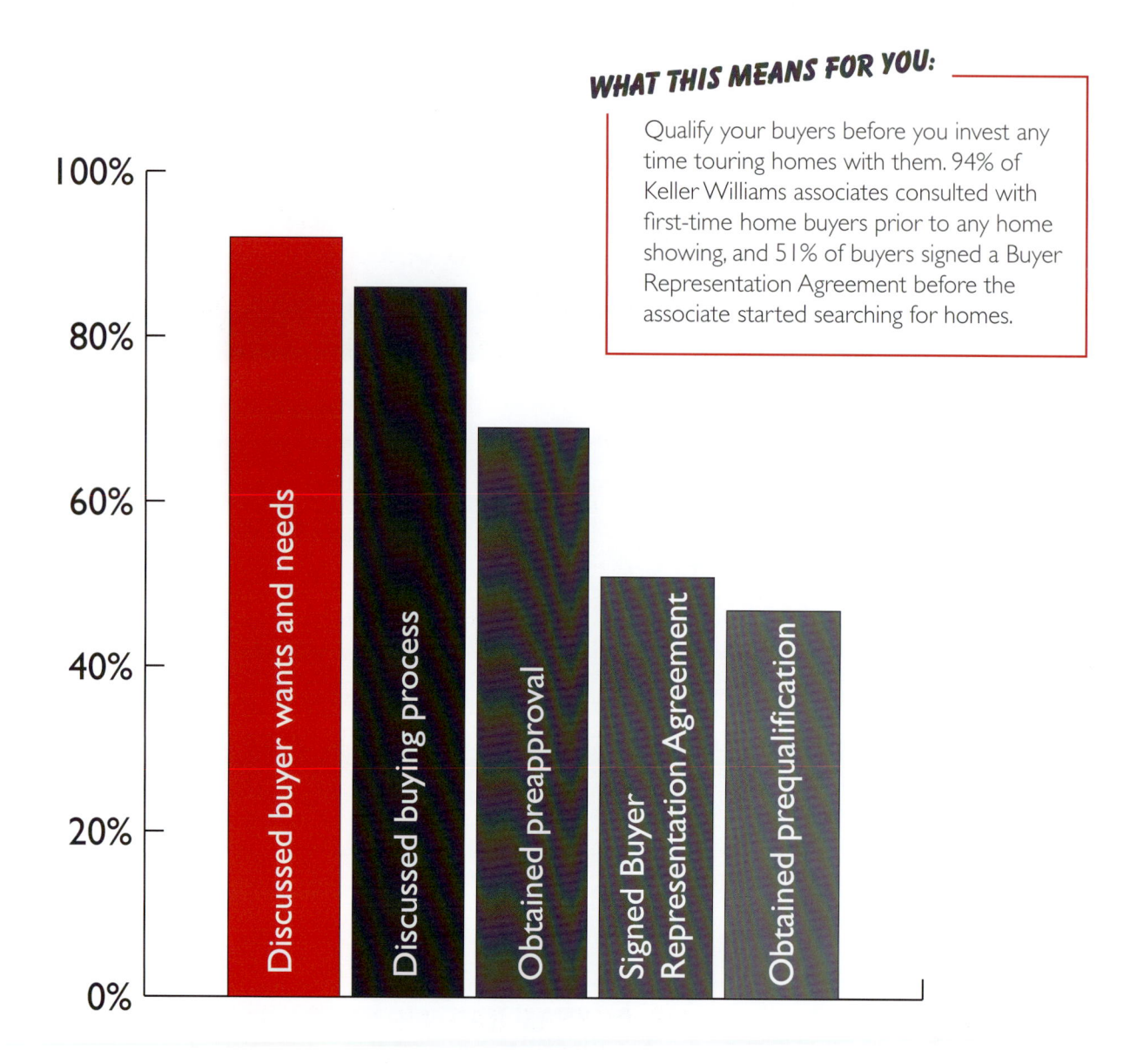

WHAT THIS MEANS FOR YOU:

Qualify your buyers before you invest any time touring homes with them. 94% of Keller Williams associates consulted with first-time home buyers prior to any home showing, and 51% of buyers signed a Buyer Representation Agreement before the associate started searching for homes.

- Discussed buyer wants and needs
- Discussed buying process
- Obtained preapproval
- Signed Buyer Representation Agreement
- Obtained prequalification

PERCENTAGE OF AGENTS WHO DO A CONSULTATION WITH THEIR FIRST-TIME HOME BUYERS

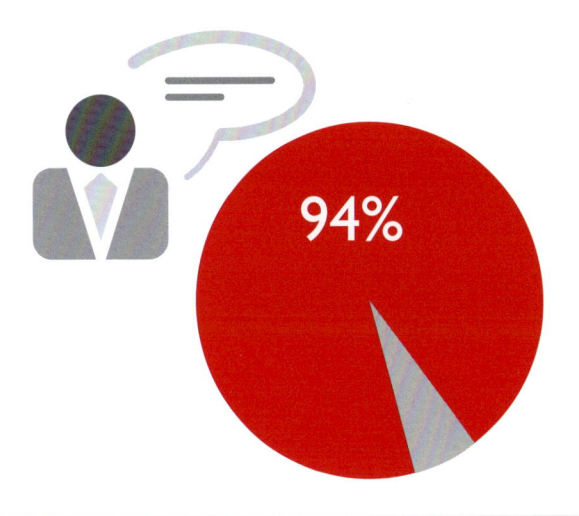

94%

MOST FIRST-TIME HOME BUYER CONSULTATIONS LASTED 30 MINS.–1 HR.

71%

MOST FIRST-TIME HOME BUYERS HAD AN ACCEPTED OFFER WITHIN THREE DAYS OF SUBMISSION

61%

5. FIRST-TIME HOME BUYERS

Home Sellers

Features That Attract Buyers 65

What's Selling 66

Top Nine Reasons Sellers Sell 66

Shipshape Sells 67

Most Common Updates 67

Condition Is Key 68

Condition: Better Is Better 69

Curb Appeal 70

Strategic Staging 71

Staging 72

Who Staged? 72

Top Ten Pricing Considerations 73

Impact of Pricing to Sell 73

When Marketing the Listing 74

Closing Costs 75

Speed of the Sale 75

Home Seller Overview

Beating the odds in a buyers' market

Not every seller will know how to make the most of a buyers' market. Pummeled with dire stories from the media about an ever-grim housing landscape, they have most likely missed the bright spots that have been slowly emerging as the market improves. Prices have essentially stabilized and inventory is slowly decreasing, meaning that there are fewer and fewer homes to compete with for a sale.

When the tax credit expired in June 2010, many sellers feared that the buyers were not coming back, yet after an initial drop in July, NAR statistics showed that—by December—home sales were actually greater (5.28 million) than they were at the beginning of the year (5.05 million) while the tax credit was still in full swing.

Sellers can still get the highest possible list-to-sell ratio and sell their homes as quickly as possible if they are willing to put their trust in two time-tested principles of real estate: condition and price. These are the only two factors they have any control over, and they are the two that buyers will care about the most. How do you achieve this? Help your sellers view the house not as their home, but rather as the future home of the buyer they need to attract. Use the statistics in this section to help your sellers get into the shoes of prospective buyers and see their home with new eyes—buyer's eyes.

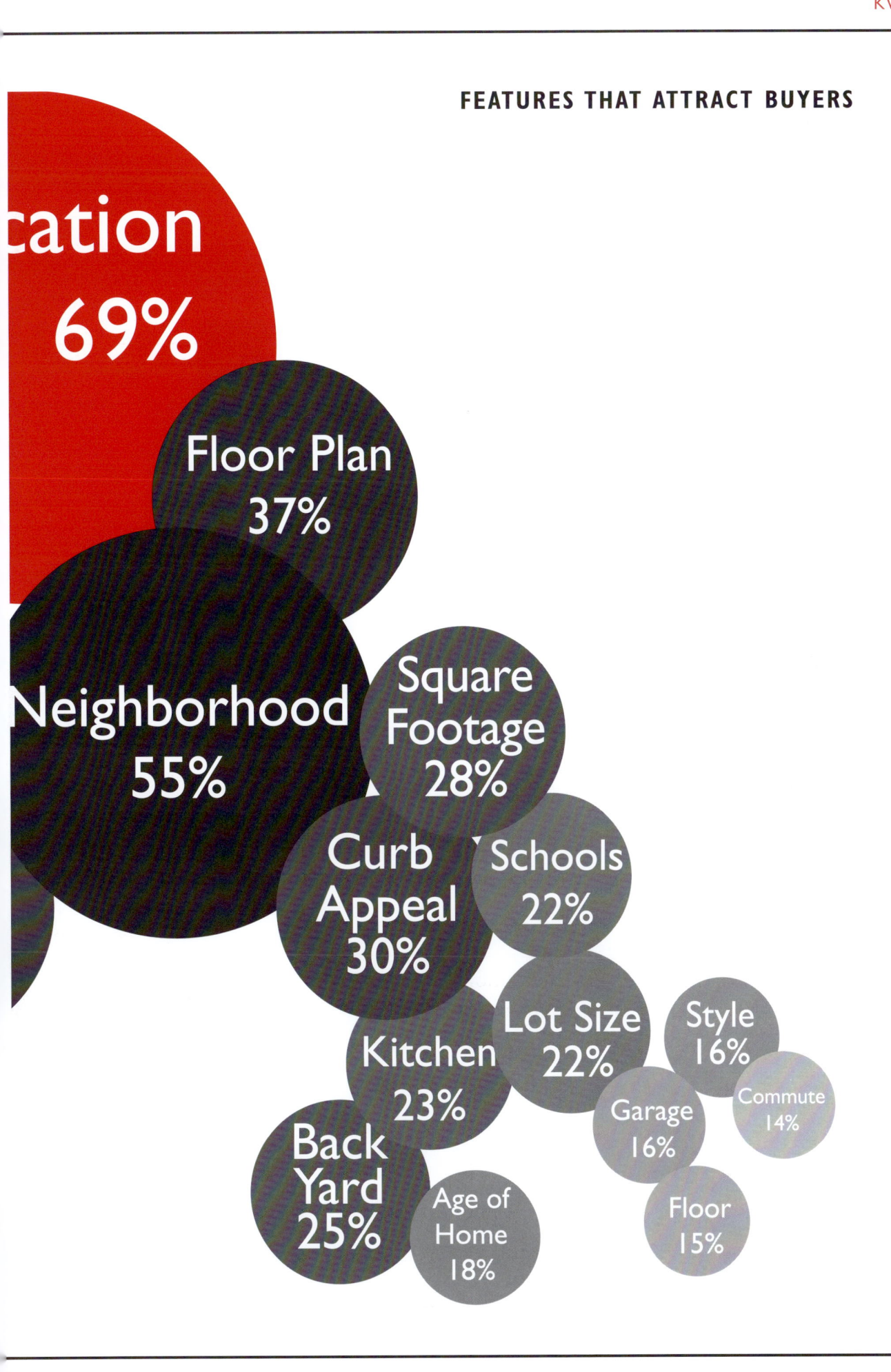

FEATURES THAT ATTRACT BUYERS

- Location 69%
- Neighborhood 55%
- Floor Plan 37%
- Curb Appeal 30%
- Square Footage 28%
- Back Yard 25%
- Kitchen 23%
- Schools 22%
- Lot Size 22%
- Age of Home 18%
- Style 16%
- Garage 16%
- Floor 15%
- Commute 14%

6. HOME SELLERS

KW MARKET NAVIGATOR 2011

WHAT'S SELLING

- 72% Traditional Transactions
- 20% Distressed Property
- 4% Luxury
- 4% Estate Sale

FOR SALE

TOP NINE REASONS SELLERS SELL

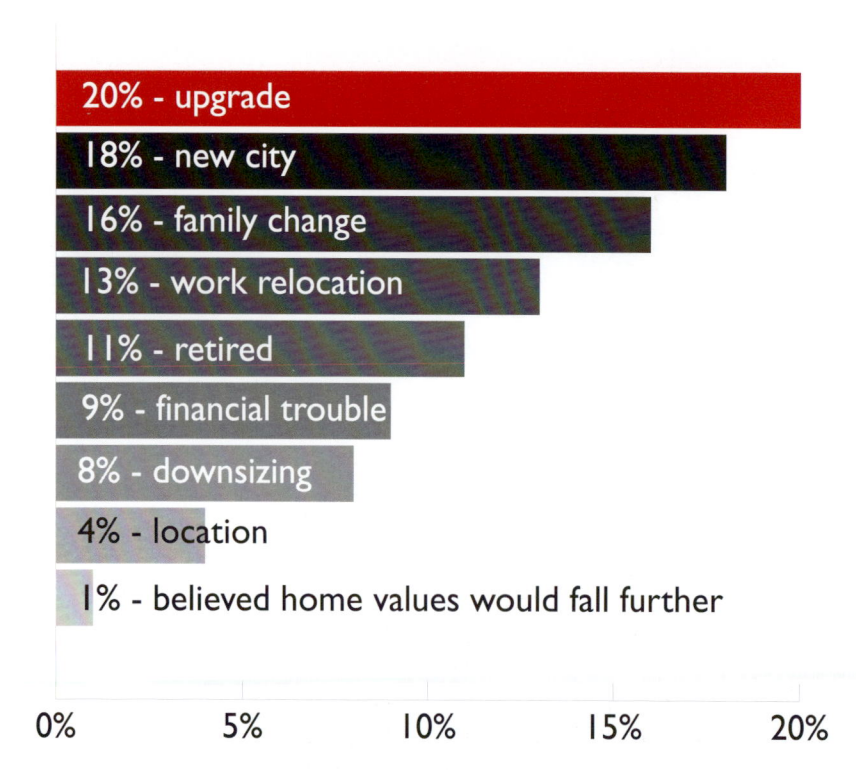

- 20% - upgrade
- 18% - new city
- 16% - family change
- 13% - work relocation
- 11% - retired
- 9% - financial trouble
- 8% - downsizing
- 4% - location
- 1% - believed home values would fall further

WHAT THIS MEANS FOR YOU:

Only 1 in 5 respondents indicated a high degree of urgency to sell. Counsel your buyers that there may be fewer concessions, buy-downs, or price reductions when sellers have lower levels of urgency.

KW RESEARCH

SHIPSHAPE SELLS

Repeat buyers, in particular move-up buyers, are looking for a home in great condition, with 49% of them buying a home in excellent condition and another 40% buying a home in good condition. If your sellers live in a neighborhood that attracts move-up buyers, be sure the home is in tip-top condition and stands out from the rest by getting the home preinspected!

8% Sellers had a prelisting inspection before listing

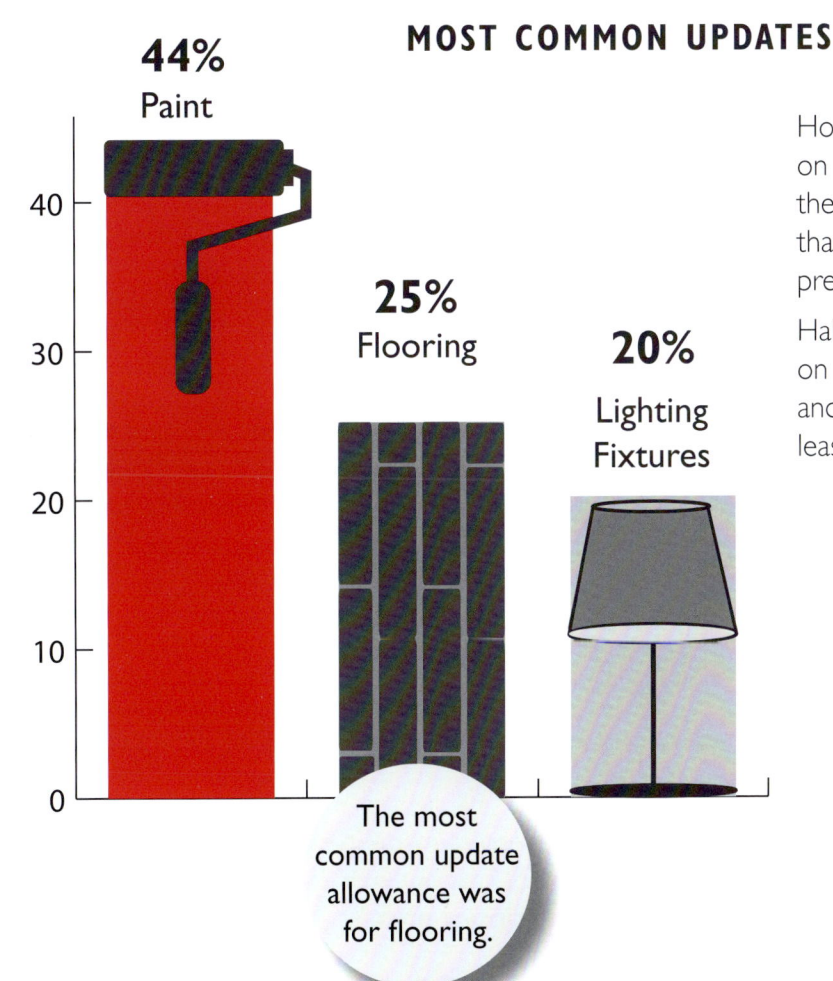

MOST COMMON UPDATES

44% Paint
25% Flooring
20% Lighting Fixtures

Home sellers typically spent more on general home updating while they lived in the home ($8,939) than they did in making updates to prepare the home to sell ($3,378).

Half of sellers spent at least $100 on updates in preparation to sell and a quarter of sellers spent at least $2,000.

The most common update allowance was for flooring.

6. HOME SELLERS

75% Homes sold either fairly updated or very updated

75% Started repairing the home to sell 1–8 weeks before listing

CONDITION IS KEY

vs.

94%
Homes in better condition were **offered** a higher percent of the list price

88%
Homes in poor condition were **offered** a lower percent of the list price

96%
Homes in better condition **sold** for an average of 96% of the list price

92%
Homes in poor condition **sold** for an average of 92% of the list price. On a $200,000 home, that's a difference of $8,000 less than homes in better condition!

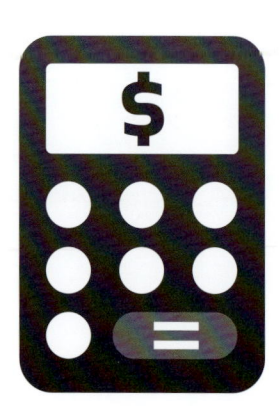

- The most common repairs made in preparation to sell were to the *roof* or the *plumbing*.
- The most common repair as a concession or allowance was the *plumbing* or *electrical*.
- The average cost of repairs made in preparation to sell was $2,444.55, with 75% of respondents spending $1,700 or less, or 1.33% of the final closing price.

CONDITION: BETTER IS BETTER

Homes in good or excellent condition will attract the most buyers, and command higher prices. Homes in better condition sold for an average of 96% of the list price compared to homes in poorer condition which sold for an average of 92% of the list price.

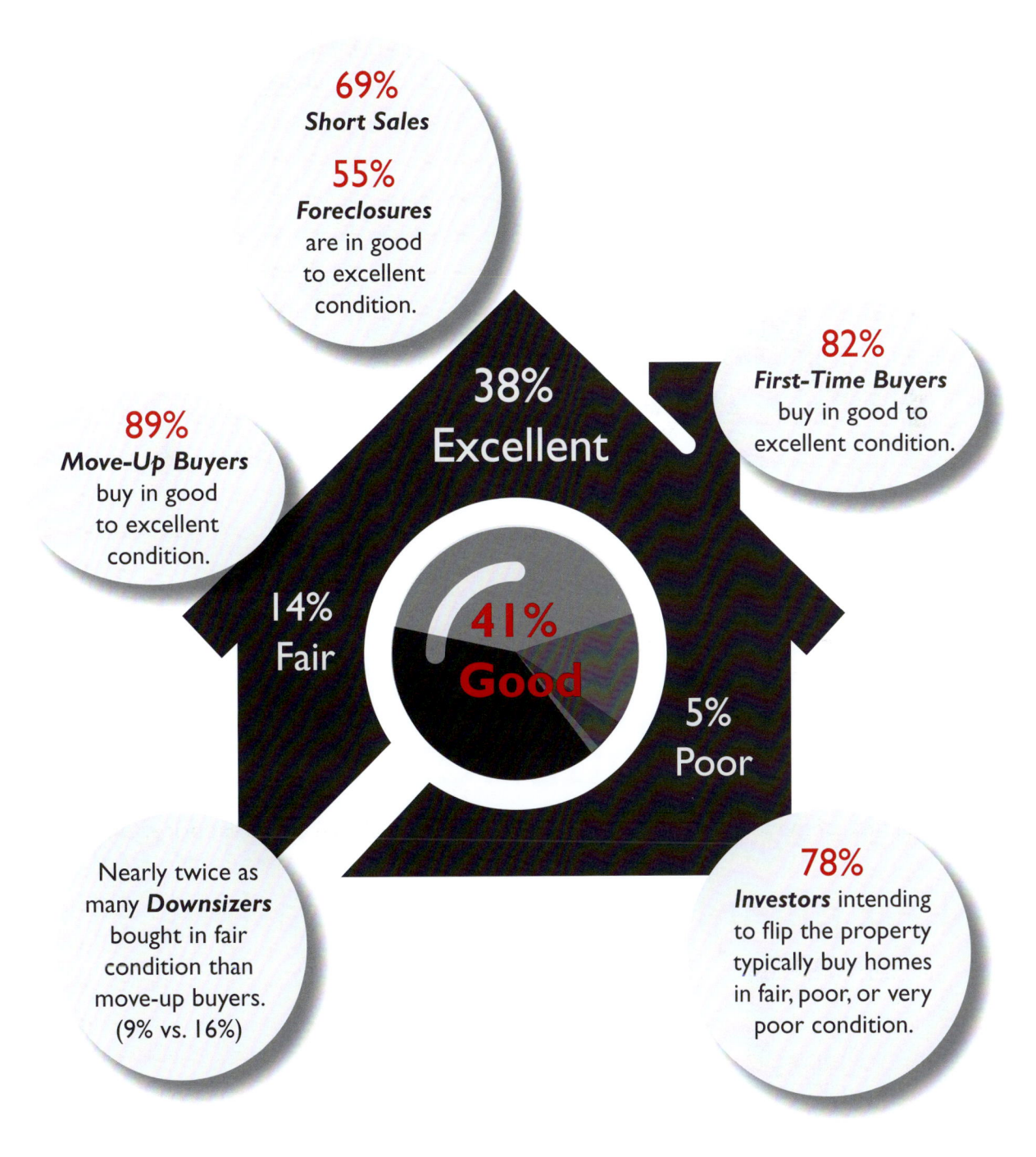

69% *Short Sales*

55% *Foreclosures* are in good to excellent condition.

82% *First-Time Buyers* buy in good to excellent condition.

89% *Move-Up Buyers* buy in good to excellent condition.

38% Excellent
14% Fair
41% Good
5% Poor

Nearly twice as many *Downsizers* bought in fair condition than move-up buyers. (9% vs. 16%)

78% *Investors* intending to flip the property typically buy homes in fair, poor, or very poor condition.

CURB APPEAL

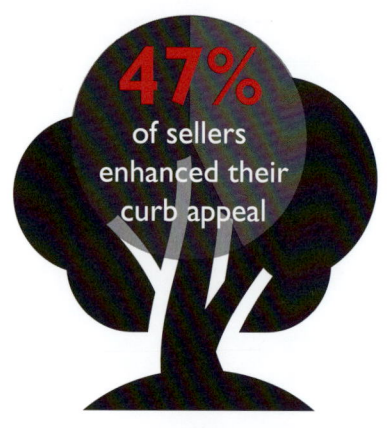

47% of sellers enhanced their curb appeal

Among those who enhanced their curb appeal, most spent between $150 and $1,000 and started up to five weeks in advance.

Sellers who enhanced curb appeal:

- Had good or excellent results compared to only 68% of homes without enhancements
- Received their first offer **6** days faster
- Sold **7** days faster
- For **1.23** percentage points higher in the list-to-sell percent

Trimming trees and bushes 73%

Door hardware 11% Power washing 40% Mulch 54%
New plants 51% Window washing 44%
Fresh exterior paint 23%

STRATEGIC STAGING

ROOMS THAT WERE STAGED

- 73% Living Room
- 64% Kitchen
- 58% Master Bedroom
- 49% Dining Room
- 45% Master Bath
- 37% All Rooms
- 16% Office

WHAT THIS MEANS FOR YOU:

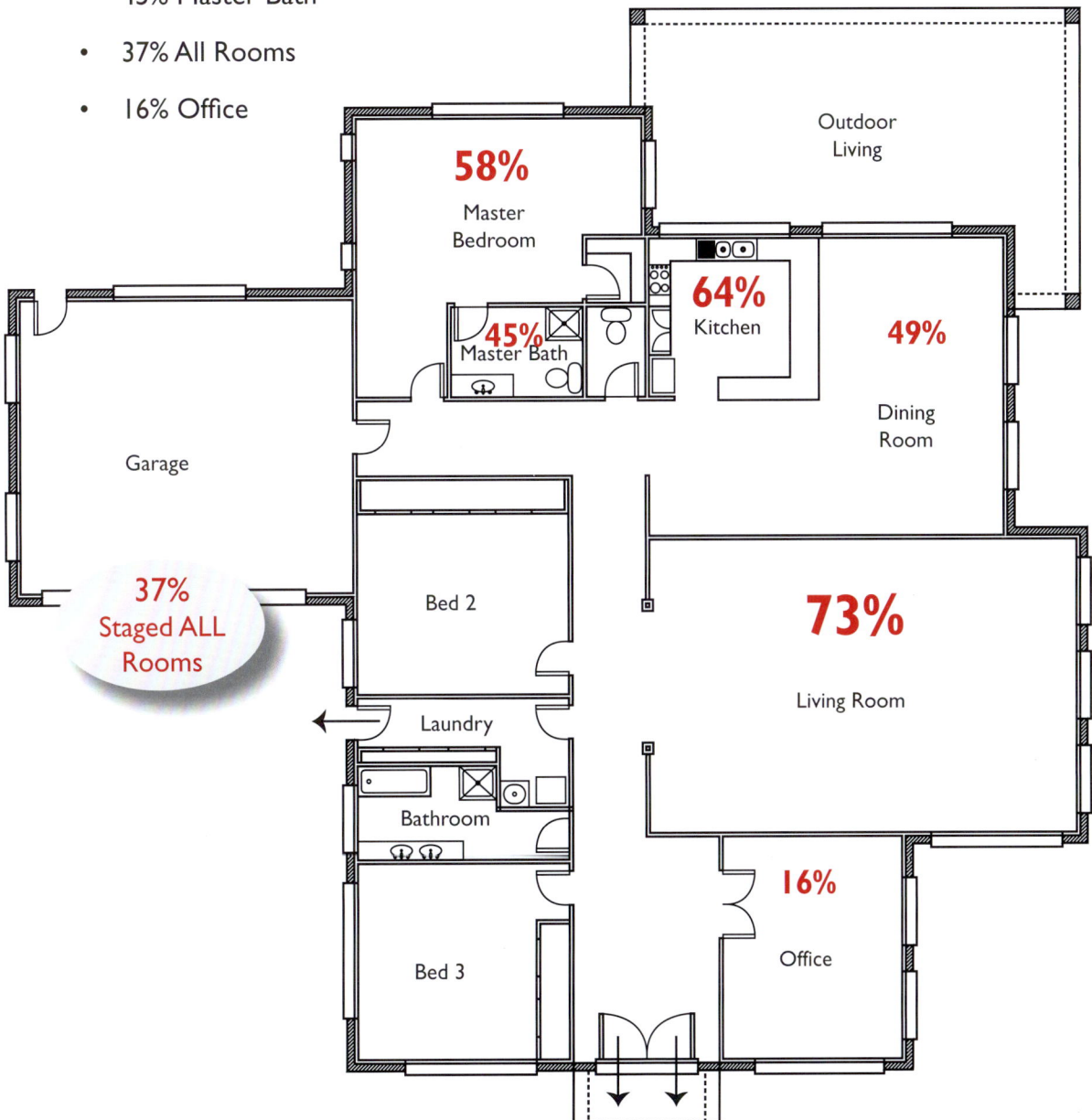

Encourage your sellers to stage. The typical seller only spent about 7 hours and $250 staging their home to sell, and had approximately two more showings and sold for 1.7 percentage points higher in the list-to-sell ratio.

58% Master Bedroom
45% Master Bath
64% Kitchen
49% Dining Room
37% Staged ALL Rooms
73% Living Room
16% Office

Outdoor Living
Garage
Bed 2
Laundry
Bathroom
Bed 3

STAGING

DO THE MATH!

If your seller spends a median of $250 on staging and the selling price of a staged home is typically 1.7% higher, then for a $200,000 home, staging can result in a $3,150 return on investment at closing. Since only one in three sellers staged their home, the other two left money on the table!

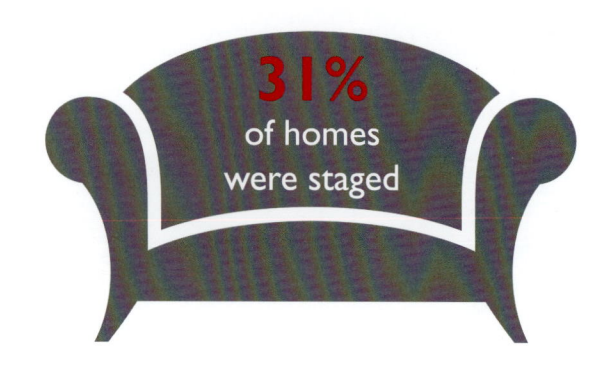

Cost of staging remained minimal. Those who hired a staging professional typically paid between $112–$562 for the service, with a median of $250.

31% of homes were staged

WHO STAGED?

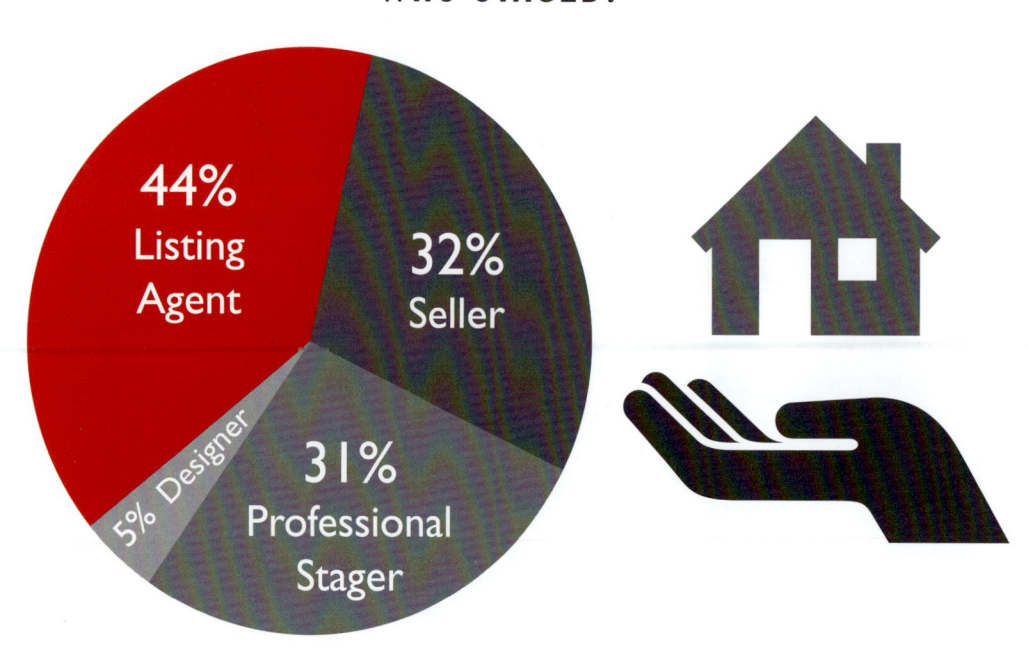

- 44% Listing Agent
- 32% Seller
- 31% Professional Stager
- 5% Designer

TOP TEN PRICING CONSIDERATIONS

1. Buyer motivation - 75%
2. Condition of home - 73%
3. School district - 66%
4. Updates/Upgrades - 62%
5. Seller motivation - 59%
6. Location - 59%
7. Features of home - 54%
8. Recently sold comps - 54%
9. Inventory - 44%
10. Price per square foot - 41%

WHAT THIS MEANS FOR YOU:

Of the top ten pricing considerations, sellers only have control over three: condition, updates, and price per square foot. Work with your sellers to establish the most competitive price, and recommend any necessary improvements before the home goes in the MLS.

- Of those who reduced the list price, they typically waited an average of six weeks to reduce it.

- The typical price reduction was between $5,000–$15,000.

IMPACT OF PRICING TO SELL

48%
Priced their home according to their agent's interpretation of its market value and the listing ...

- Sold after **56** days on market compared to 105 and sold **49** days faster

- Sold for **6.7** percentage points higher in the list-to-sell ratio. For a home listed at $200,000, that resulted in a list price-to-sell ratio of 96% vs. 89%. That's a difference of $13,400!

- Sold for at least **1 less** price reduction

About the Home Sale

	Average	Median
Days on Market	85	55
Closed Price	$279,499	$217,000
List-to-Sell Ratio	92%	94%

WHEN MARKETING THE LISTING

49% Included detailed photo descriptions

31% Included a virtual tour online

The best tactics for getting a listing sold other than through the MLS:

1. Placement on real estate sites such as Realtor.com, Trulia, Zillow (22%)
2. Web listings with virtual tour (19%)
3. Signage (for-sale signs, rider and directional signs, balloons) (18%)

CLOSING COSTS

- **43%** of all buyers received some closings costs from the seller. Of those who did receive closing costs, on average they received 2.6% of the sales price or $4,700.

- **75%** of those who received closing costs received at least $3,000 (or 1.56% of the sales price)

SPEED OF THE SALE

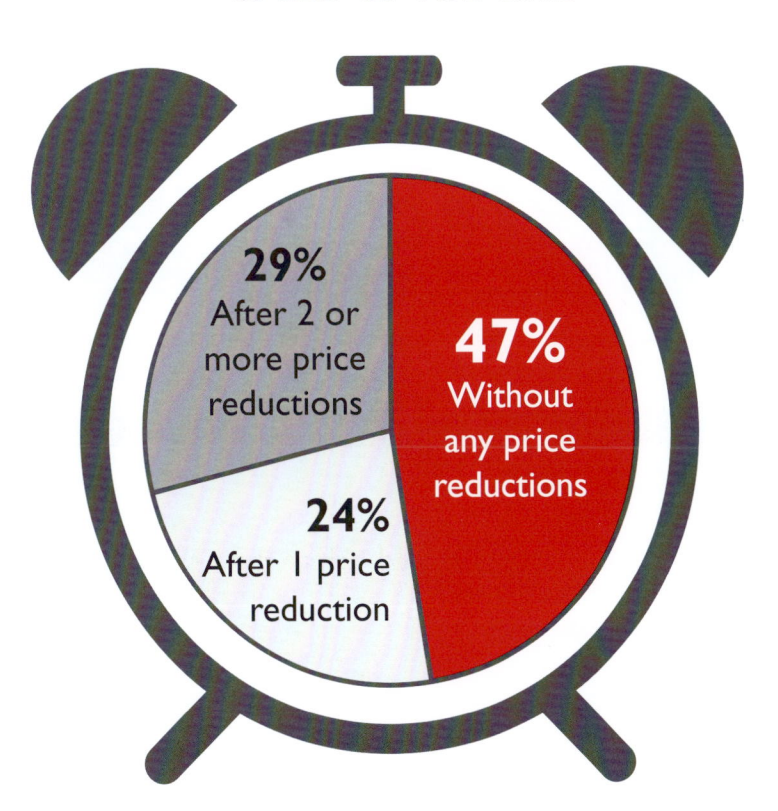

- **29%** After 2 or more price reductions
- **47%** Without any price reductions
- **24%** After 1 price reduction

Distressed Properties

AGENT INVOLVEMENT	78
MOTIVATING FACTORS	78
AGENTS' KEY CHALLENGES WITH DISTRESSED PROPERTIES	79
COMMON SHORT SALE SCENARIOS	80
THE DOWNWARD SPIRAL OF DEFAULTS AND HOME PRICES	81
COUNSEL PATIENCE FOR YOUR DISTRESSED PROPERTY BUYERS	83
EARLY STAGE "SOS" TO LENDER	83
LAG TIME IN CONTACTING LENDER	84
LENDER RECOURSE: DEFICIENCY JUDGMENT	85
ASSESSING RISK OF LENDER SEEKING DEFICIENCY JUDGMENT	85
DISTRESSED PROPERTY SALES SUCCESS FACTORS	86
SHORT SALE CHECKLIST	87
TYPICAL DISTRESSED PROPERTY TIME LINE	88

Distressed Properties

Overview and Opportunities

Bank-owned foreclosures (REO) and short sales both present great value opportunity for buyers. Prices can be as much as 30% below market in some areas—and in others, distressed properties are the market. Either way, experts agree there's value for a buyer who wants to own five years or more. Rental rates are advancing too—great news for investors who want to buy and rent. REO transactions move quickly; short sales are still slow, but they are getting faster. These buyers need patience to get what they want—and a good agent to keep them in the deal until it's done.

AGENT INVOLVEMENT

71%
Associates have worked with a distressed property buyer in the past year

MOTIVATING FACTORS

Factor	Percentage
Affordable Price	60%
Mortgage Rates	39%
Can Afford to Buy	30%
Family Situation Changed	15%
Location, School	14%
Steady Job	13%
Inventory	13%
Space	12%
Equity	11%

Average Activity of Agents Who Worked with Distressed Properties		
Over a Sixth-Month Period	Short Sale	REO
Properties Shown to All Buyers	20	20
Offers Written with All Buyers	7	9
Contracts Closed with All Buyers	4	5

AGENTS' KEY CHALLENGES WITH DISTRESSED PROPERTIES

1.	Banks operate differently than individual sellers	**57%**
2.	Longer time lines	**56%**
3.	Helping the buyer be patient	**54%**
4.	Working with an unresponsive listing agent	**42%**
5.	Increased paperwork	**40%**
6.	Increased chances for multiple offers	**35%**
7.	How to navigate the banks' chain of command	**35%**
8.	Being patient	**33%**
9.	Help buyer see they are not a steal	**21%**

55% of agents representing short sale sellers indicated the average negotiation time with the banks during the course of the short sale has decreased during the past six months. 33% indicated that it has stayed the same.

COMMON SHORT SALE SCENARIOS

The most common reason homeowners went into default was because they were unable to continue making payments due to a sudden change in their financial situation. 18% were unable to continue making payments due to a nonemergency change in financial condition, and the other 18% were underwater and decided to walk even though they were able to still make payments.

The distressed property crisis had its origins in bad loans and overinflated prices in the early and mid-2000s. That's changing—now most defaults and foreclosures are happening because of stubbornly high unemployment in many metro areas and regions.

Homeowner Math: Why They Walk Away		
Value at original purchase	$200,000	
Current value (40% market decline)	$120,000	
Time to regain original value at 4% annual appreciation	After 14 years $208,000	Even with foreclosure, they may be able to buy again in 5–7 years.
Cost to purchase a home after 7 years	$161,000 ($158,000 plus assumed 2% closing costs)	The 7 years may also have provided time for the consumer to save for a larger down payment than they originally had.

THE DOWNWARD SPIRAL OF DEFAULTS AND HOME PRICES

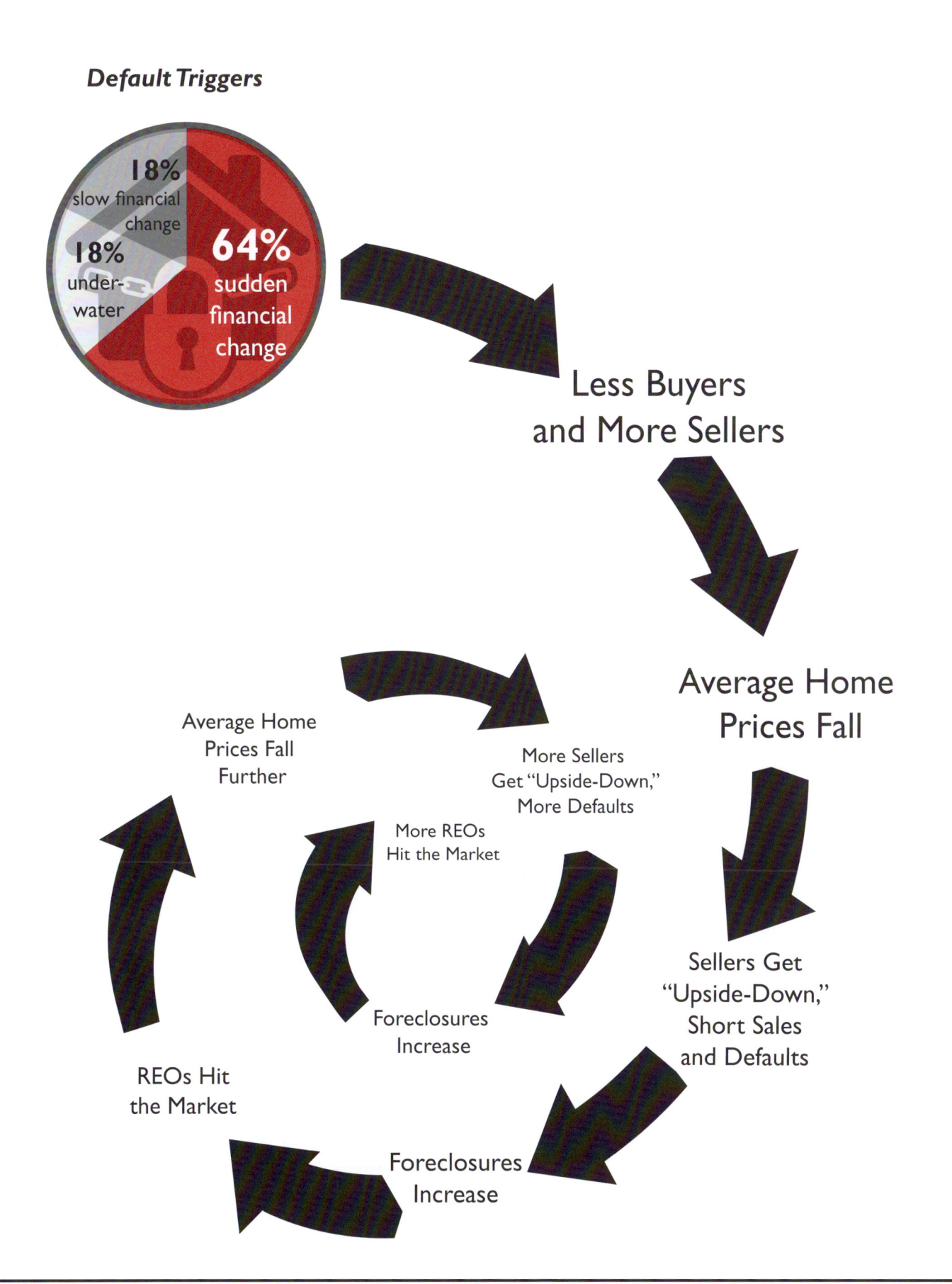

Default Triggers

- 18% slow financial change
- 18% underwater
- 64% sudden financial change

Less Buyers and More Sellers

Average Home Prices Fall

Sellers Get "Upside-Down," Short Sales and Defaults

Foreclosures Increase

REOs Hit the Market

Average Home Prices Fall Further

More Sellers Get "Upside-Down," More Defaults

More REOs Hit the Market

Foreclosures Increase

7. Distressed Properties

Advantages of Short Sale vs. Foreclosure		
	Short Sale	Foreclosure
Credit score damage (based on agent reports)	150 points or less (Note: Credit-monitoring agencies may change policy on score modification.)	250 points or more
Mark against your financial record	Drops off scoring system after 7 years	Permanent record at the county courthouse
Time to qualify to buy again (FNMA)	2 years	5–7 years
Down payment on future purchase (FNMA)	Less than 10%	10% or greater; maybe 20%

Short sale sellers typically first met with their agent about a month after they missed their first payment (median = 34.5 days). The most common reason they waited was because they were seeking a loan modification. Other common reasons were that they didn't know their options or they were embarrassed and fearful. 17% were in a state of denial.

WHAT THIS MEANS FOR YOU:

Agents say most distressed homeowners want to try a loan modification, but the success rate of modifications is very low—between 3%–6%. Those that fail usually become short sale candidates.

KW RESEARCH

COUNSEL PATIENCE FOR YOUR DISTRESSED PROPERTY BUYERS

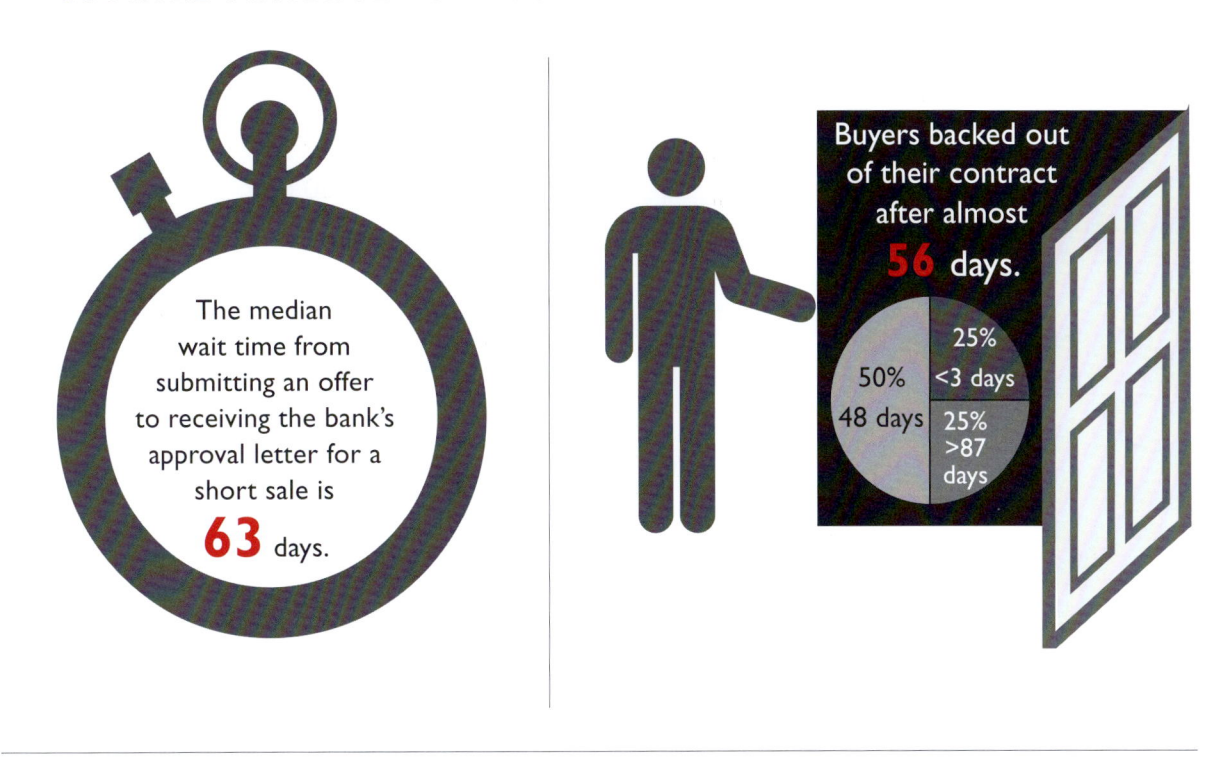

The median wait time from submitting an offer to receiving the bank's approval letter for a short sale is **63** days.

Buyers backed out of their contract after almost **56** days.

- 25% <3 days
- 50% 48 days
- 25% >87 days

EARLY STAGE "SOS" TO LENDER

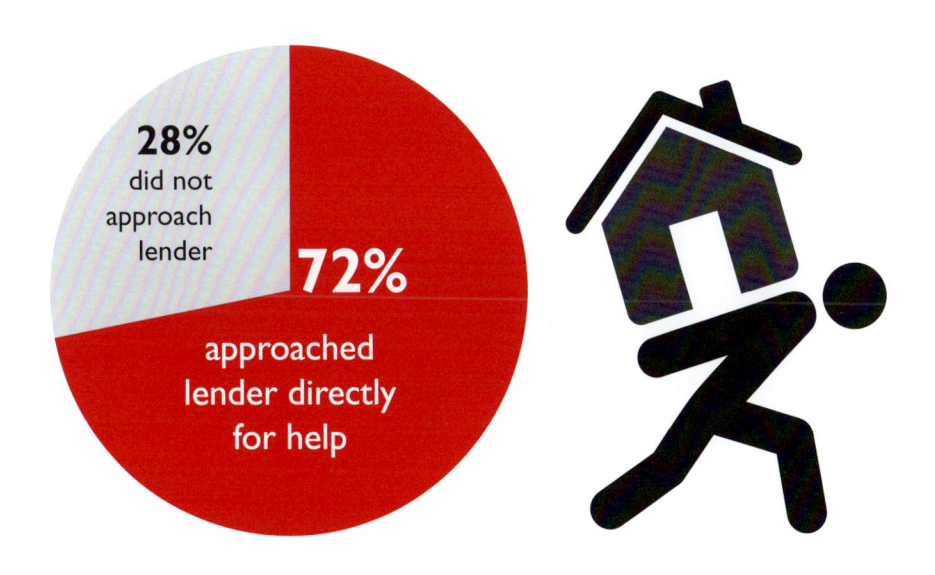

- **28%** did not approach lender
- **72%** approached lender directly for help

7. DISTRESSED PROPERTIES

KW MARKET NAVIGATOR 2011

LAG TIME IN CONTACTING LENDER

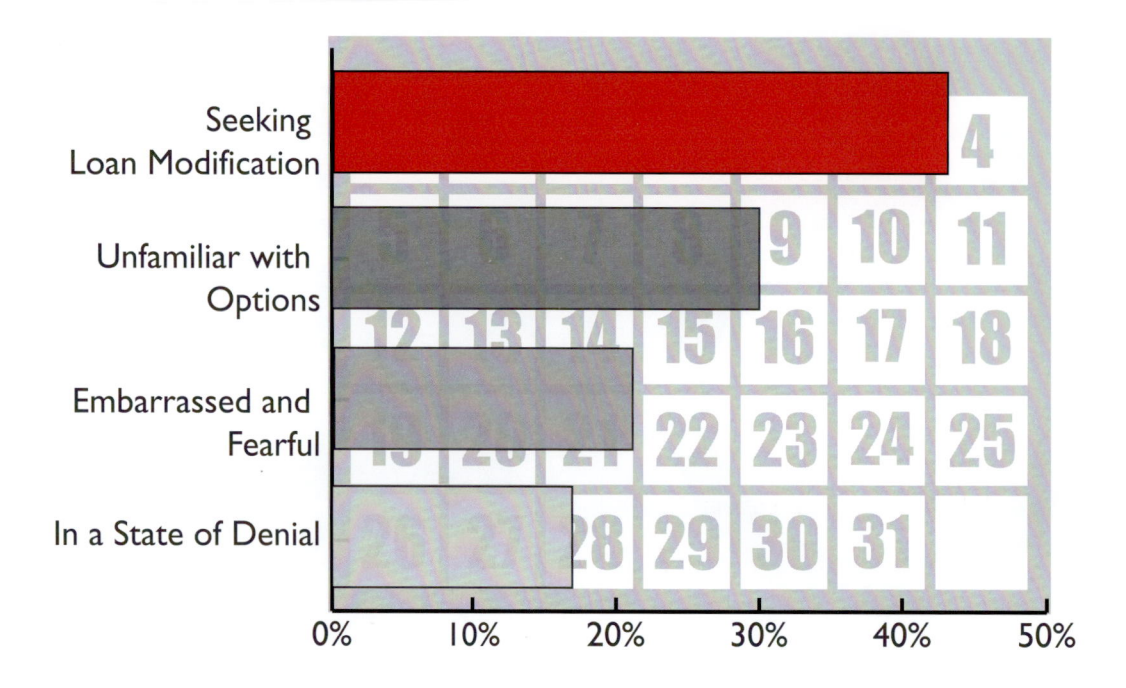

- Seeking Loan Modification: ~43%
- Unfamiliar with Options: ~30%
- Embarrassed and Fearful: ~21%
- In a State of Denial: ~17%

Buyers backing out of contracts remain a problem in short sales, but things are improving—the wait is getting shorter with most lenders. A highly skilled short sale agent gives sellers and buyers the best assurance of success. 19% of associates reported losing a buyer of a short sale listing in the past six months because the buyer walked away from the deal before receiving a response from the bank/lender, while most associates (75%) had this happen 26% of the time or less.

LENDER RECOURSE: DEFICIENCY JUDGMENT

A deficiency judgment is a claim against the borrower whose sale did not produce sufficient funds to cover what they owe on their mortgage loan. Whether a lender has recourse to levy a deficiency judgment varies from state to state. Some states do bar these judgments, but the ban only applies to the first mortgage and not to second mortgages or other liens against the property.

- The bank/lender sought a deficiency judgment for the deficient amount of the purchase money for 4% of short sale sellers.

- The bank/lender sought a deficiency judgment for the nonpurchase money or second mortgage equity line of credit for 6% of short sale sellers.

- For 66% of short sale sellers, the bank/lender did not seek a deficiency judgment.

- Seller concerned/intimidated about the perceived threat of deficiency judgments: 74% were at least moderately concerned about deficiency judgments. 13% showed no concern at all.

ASSESSING RISK OF LENDER SEEKING DEFICIENCY JUDGMENT

64% of short sale sellers were unfamiliar with deficiency judgments when they first met their agent.

85% of short sale sellers were unsure if their state law protected them under a nondeficiency law.

DISTRESSED PROPERTY SALES SUCCESS FACTORS

Certificate of Success

1. Continuous follow-up with listing agent — 59%
2. Continuous follow-up with buyer — 45%
3. Completed paperwork presented in the offer — 40%
4. Set expectations early on for the buyer — 40%
5. Corresponded with the listing agent to confirm the offer requirements — 36%
6. The buyer committed to the home — 35%
7. The buyer was flexible about time lines — 27%
8. The buyer was prepared for obstacles — 26%
9. The buyer understood process — 25%

Individuals Buying Distressed Properties

	First-Time Buyers	Buy and Flip Investors	Buy and Rent Investors
Foreclosures	32%	4%	13%
Short Sales	41%	2%	10%

First-time buyers are the most common type of buyer to purchase a distressed property.

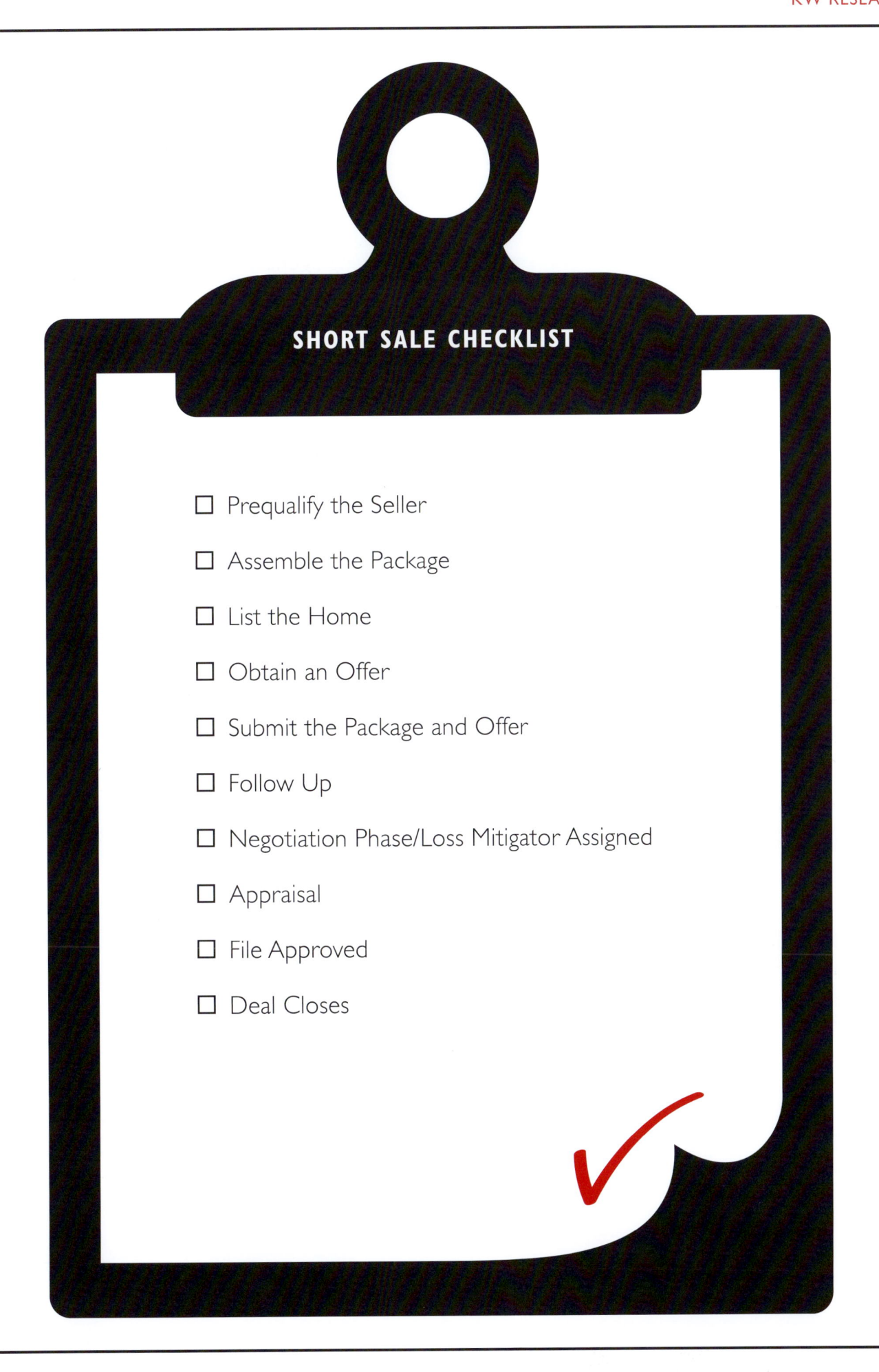

SHORT SALE CHECKLIST

- ☐ Prequalify the Seller
- ☐ Assemble the Package
- ☐ List the Home
- ☐ Obtain an Offer
- ☐ Submit the Package and Offer
- ☐ Follow Up
- ☐ Negotiation Phase/Loss Mitigator Assigned
- ☐ Appraisal
- ☐ File Approved
- ☐ Deal Closes

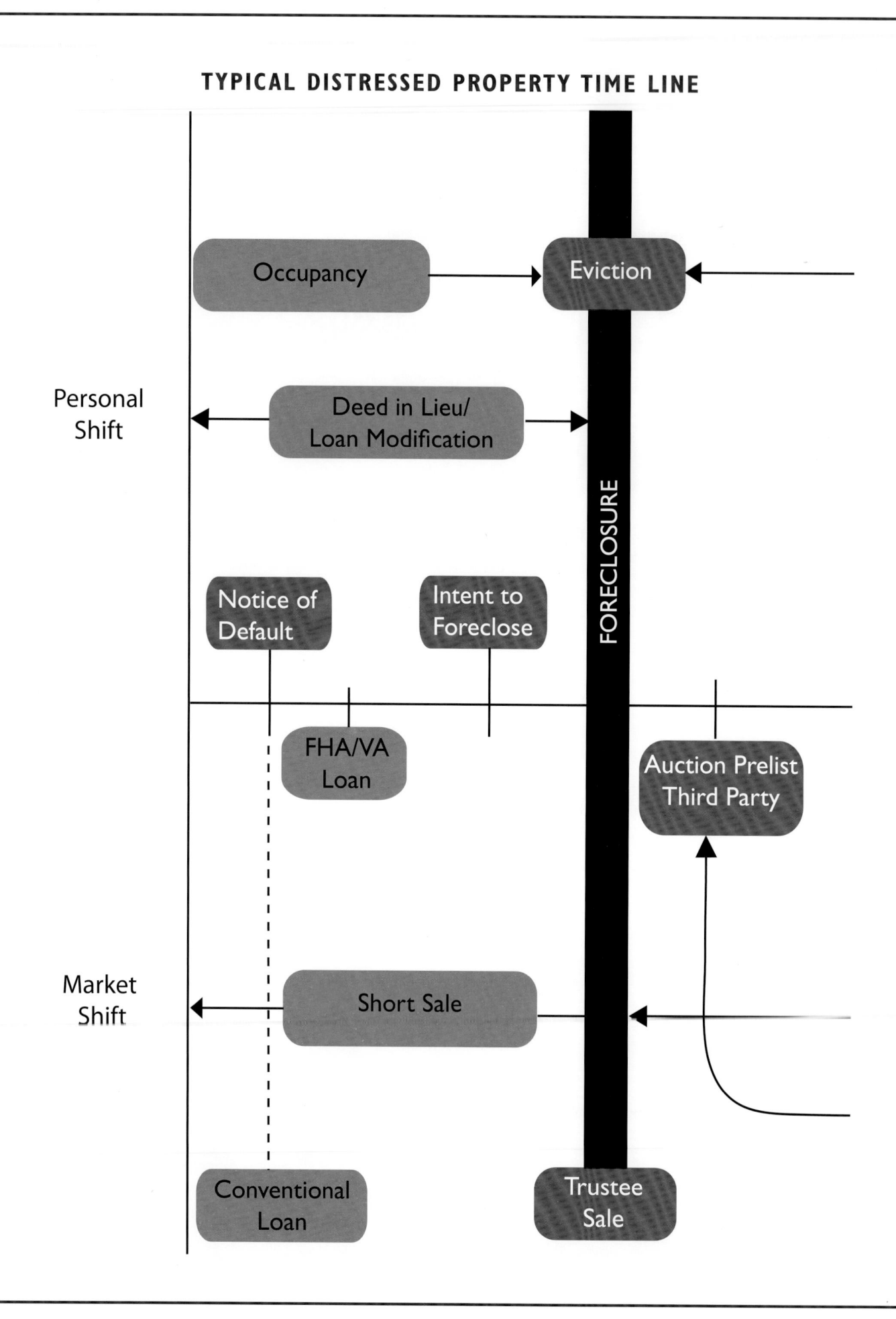

TYPICAL DISTRESSED PROPERTY TIME LINE

Personal Shift

- Occupancy → Eviction
- Deed in Lieu/ Loan Modification

FORECLOSURE

- Notice of Default
- Intent to Foreclose
- FHA/VA Loan
- Auction Prelist Third Party

Market Shift

- Short Sale
- Conventional Loan
- Trustee Sale

Redemption/
Reinstatement Period

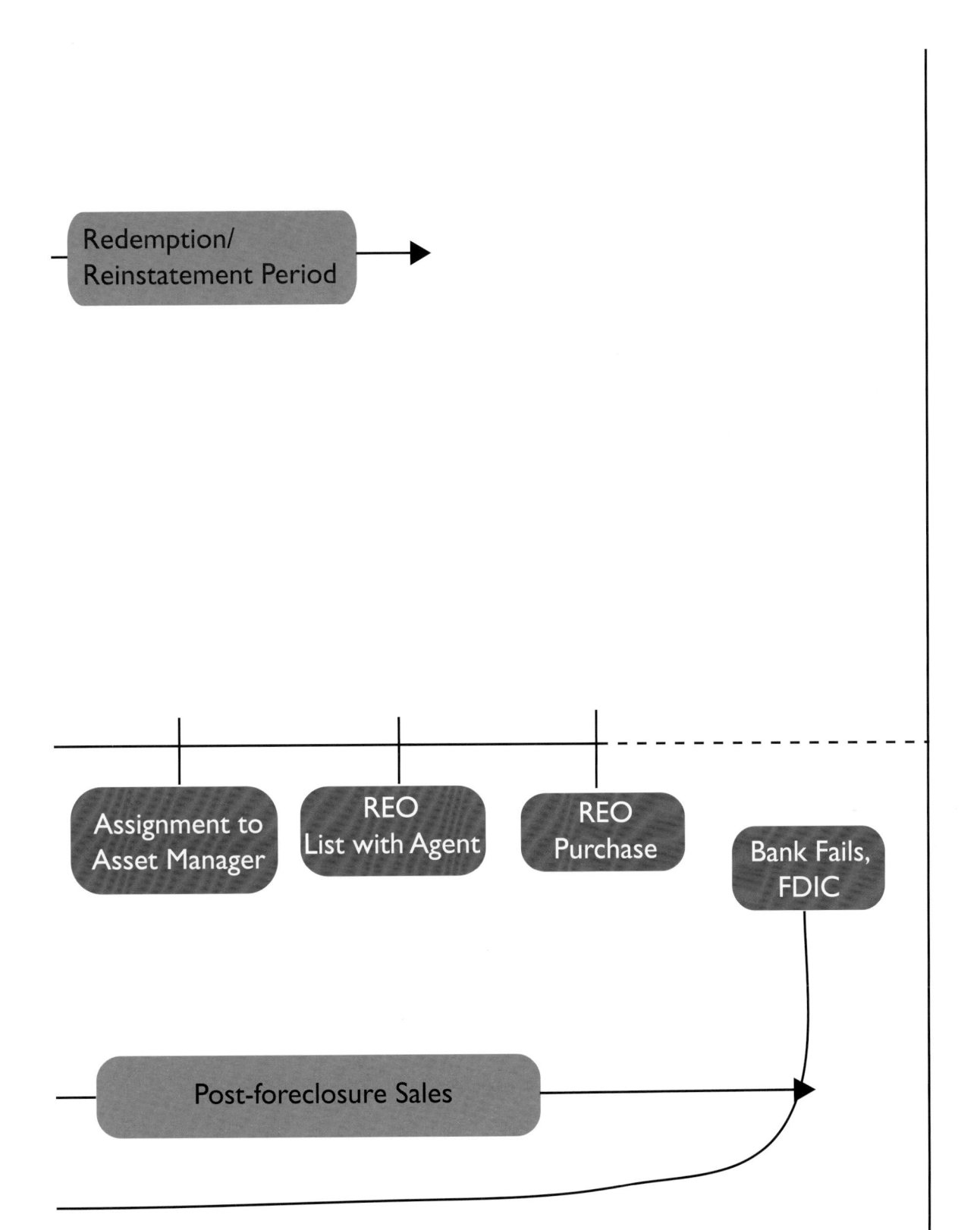

Assignment to Asset Manager → REO List with Agent → REO Purchase → Bank Fails, FDIC

Post-foreclosure Sales

7. Distressed Properties

Green Is the New Gold

1 IN 10 ASSOCIATES NOW POSITION THEMSELVES
AS GREEN SPECIALISTS 92

GREEN KNOWLEDGE 92

GREEN VALUE 92

WHAT BUYERS WANT: THREE GREEN BUCKETS 93

TAP INTO OUR GREEN COMMUNITY................................ 93

TOP THREE REASONS HOME BUYERS
WANT GREEN FEATURES.. 94

GREEN AVAILABILITY... 94

GREEN PRICES 94

FROM THE AGENT PERSPECTIVE:
WHO VALUES GREEN FEATURES THE MOST? 95

FEWER DAYS ON THE MARKET...................................... 95

GREEN GROWS 95

GREEN FEATURES BUYERS LOOK FOR MOST 96

GREEN IS NOT A FAD 96

GREEN KEYS TO SUCCESS 97

SEIZE THE OPPORTUNITY: SPECIALIZED TRAINING 97

Green Is the New Gold

Green yields higher prices, less time on market, and more business

Demand for green features has changed the real estate landscape. From residential to commercial property, our research indicates buyers want home features that are healthy, money smart, and sustainable—in other words, green. Sellers are getting higher offer prices with less time on market. That means more business opportunity in 2011, especially for well-positioned agents.

1 IN 10 ASSOCIATES NOW POSITION THEMSELVES AS GREEN SPECIALISTS

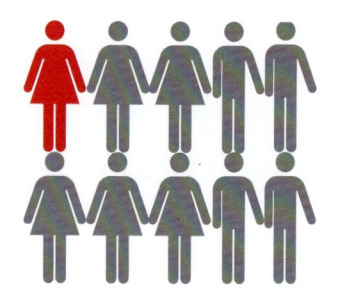

Of those

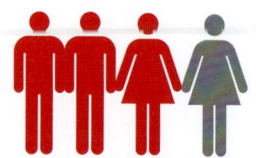

3 in 4 currently hold a specialized designation.

Another 18% said that they are planning to get one.

GREEN KNOWLEDGE

70%

report that they were at least somewhat familiar with green aspects of real estate.

GREEN VALUE

9 in 10

perceive green homes to offer more value than similar homes without the green features.

KW RESEARCH

WHAT BUYERS WANT: THREE GREEN BUCKETS

1. Healthy Considerations

2. Financial Sense

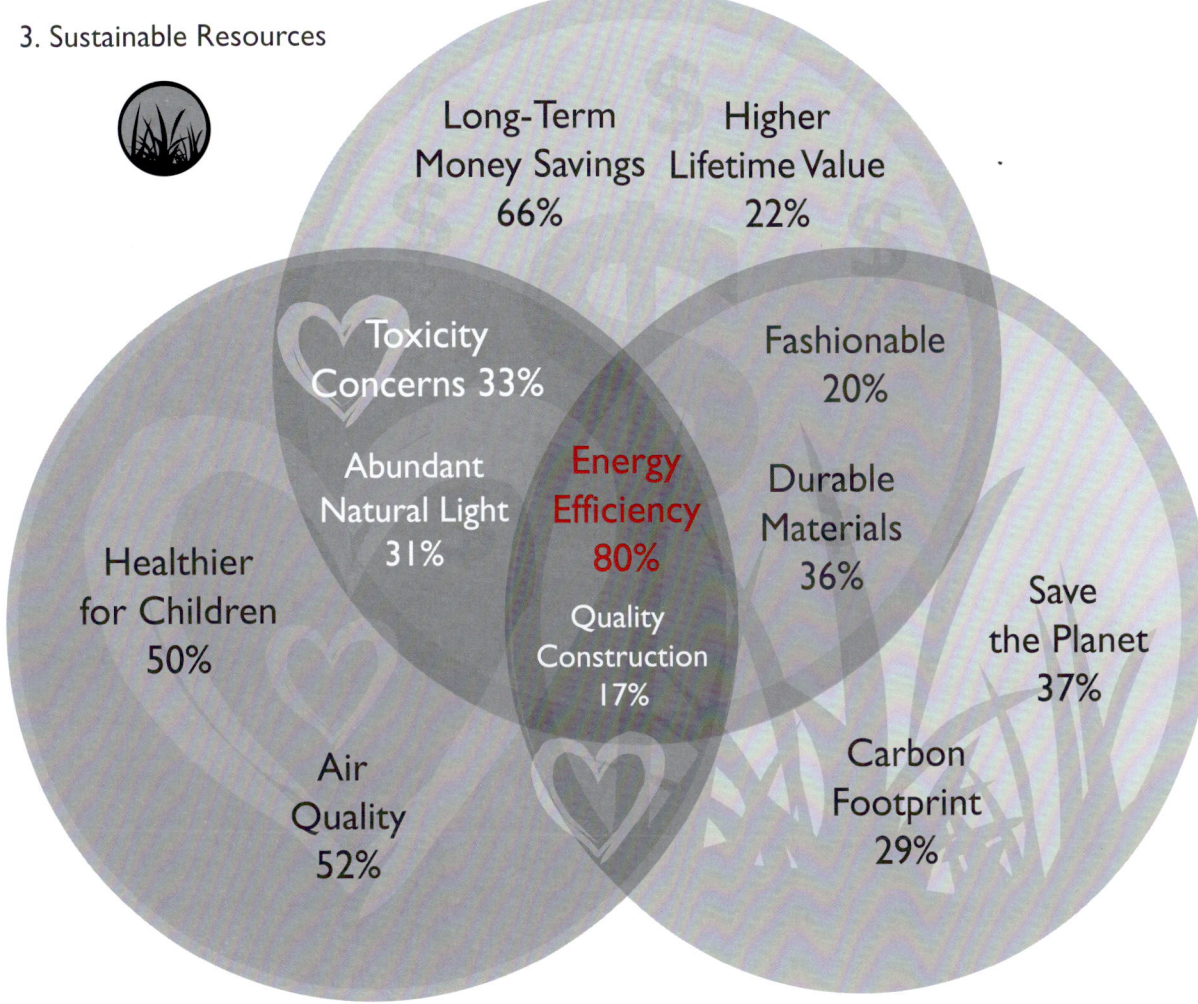

3. Sustainable Resources

8. GREEN IS THE NEW GOLD

Long-Term Money Savings 66%

Higher Lifetime Value 22%

Toxicity Concerns 33%

Fashionable 20%

Abundant Natural Light 31%

Energy Efficiency 80%

Durable Materials 36%

Healthier for Children 50%

Quality Construction 17%

Save the Planet 37%

Air Quality 52%

Carbon Footprint 29%

TAP INTO OUR GREEN COMMUNITY

Visit www.facebook.com/greenyourhome for updates and news on how you can expand your green knowledge.

KW MARKET NAVIGATOR 2011

TOP THREE REASONS HOME BUYERS WANT GREEN FEATURES

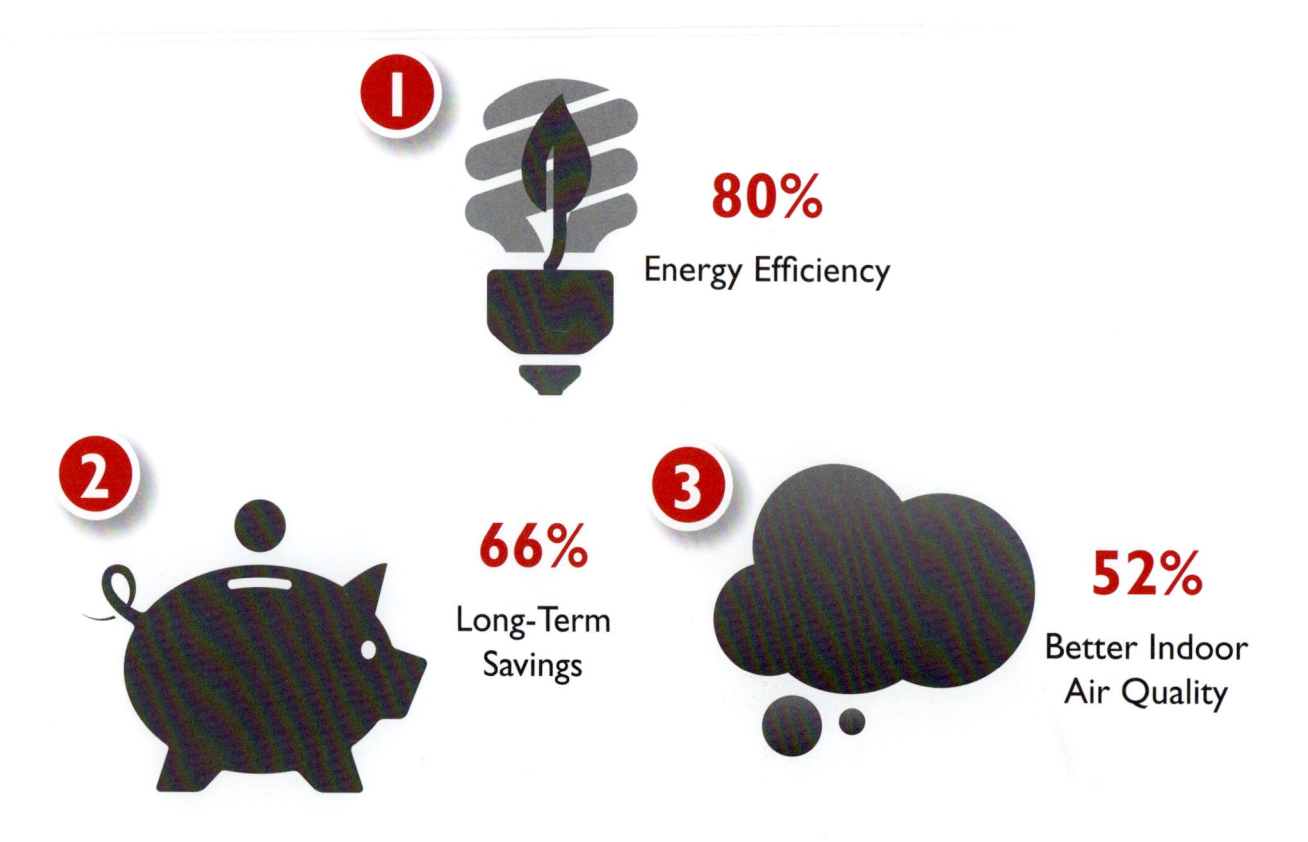

1 **80%** Energy Efficiency

2 **66%** Long-Term Savings

3 **52%** Better Indoor Air Quality

GREEN AVAILABILITY

53% indicate that homes with green features are readily available in their market.

GREEN PRICES

61% perceive higher prices for homes with green features compared to similar conventional homes.

KW RESEARCH

FROM THE AGENT PERSPECTIVE: WHO VALUES GREEN FEATURES THE MOST?

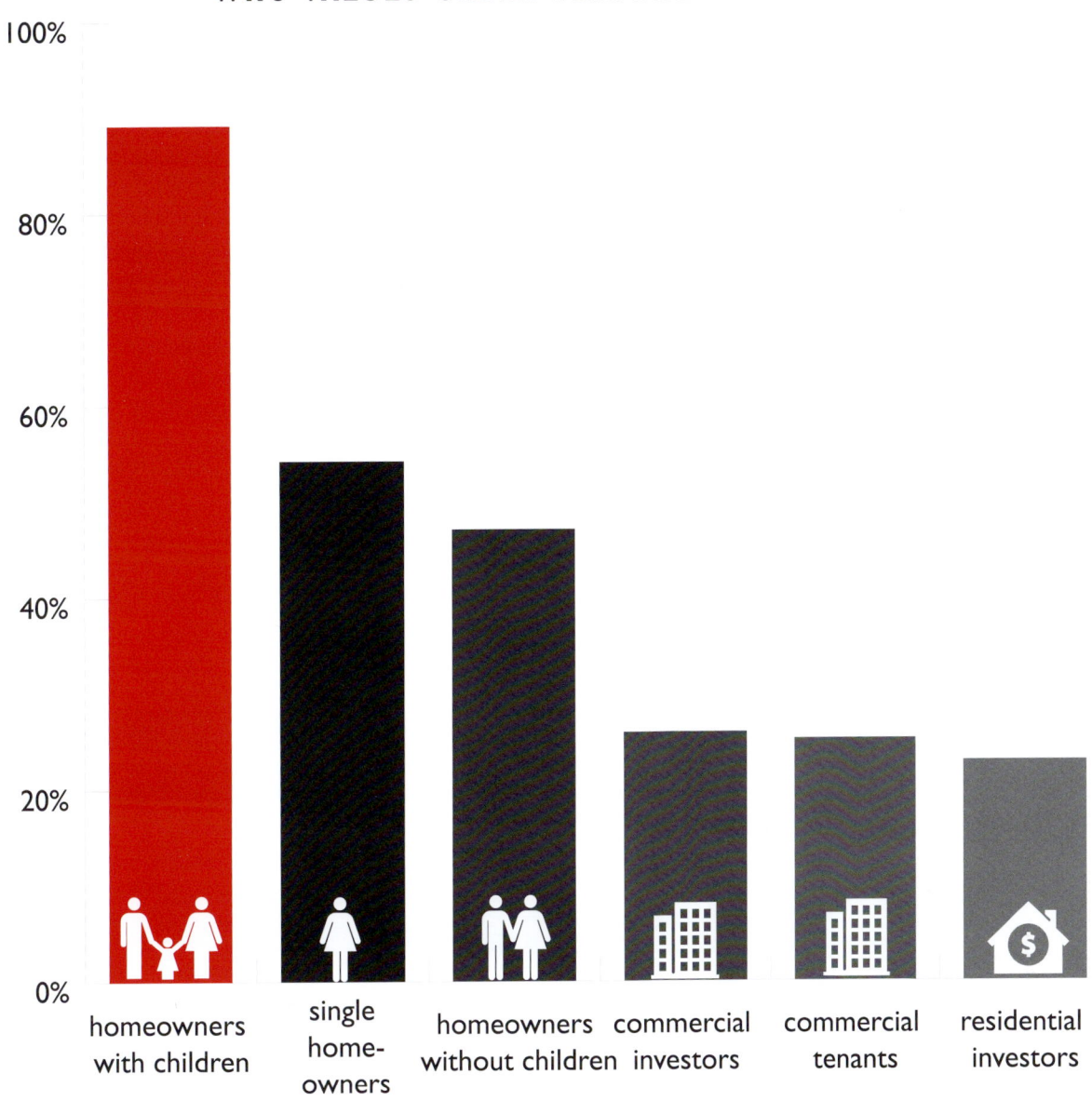

| homeowners with children | single home-owners | homeowners without children | commercial investors | commercial tenants | residential investors |

8. GREEN IS THE NEW GOLD

FEWER DAYS ON THE MARKET

52% report homes with green features spend fewer days on the market.

GREEN GROWS

Business GROWS

53% see green as a possibility to grow business.

95

GREEN IS NOT A FAD

72% of agents agree green is here to stay.

How to Succeed as a Green Agent

1. Actively participate in your local community or establish a green network.

2. Attract interested/knowledgeable buyers or inform buyers of the value.

3. Be authentic, walk the walk, and implement green practices in your life.

GREEN FEATURES BUYERS LOOK FOR MOST

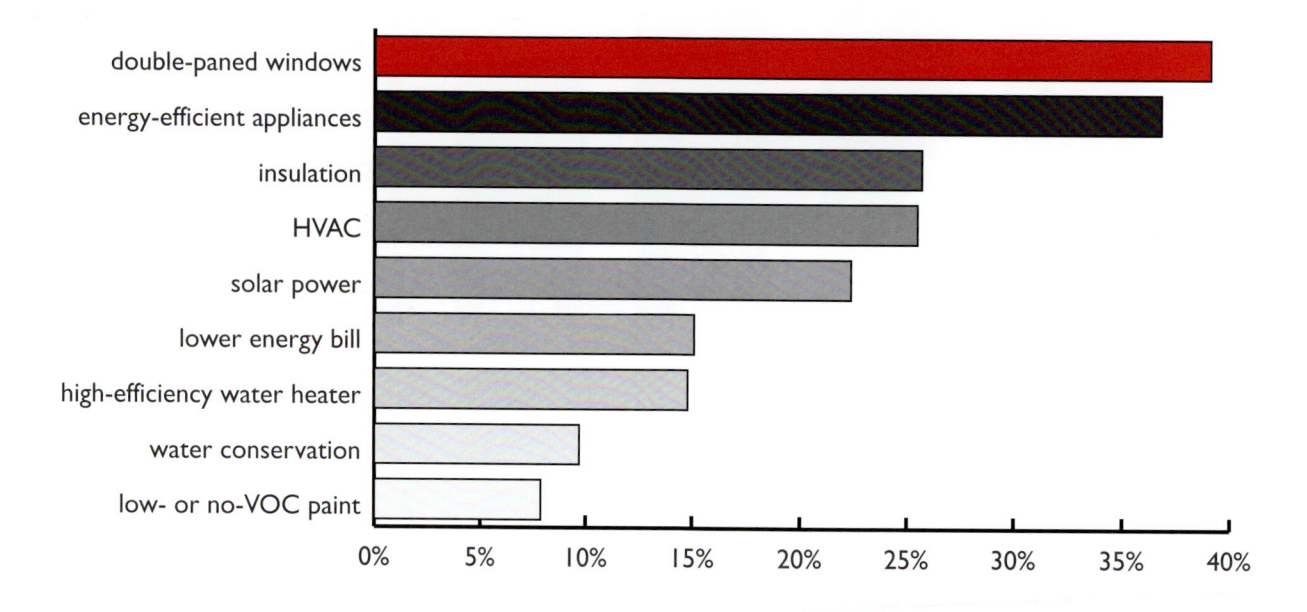

Feature	Percentage
double-paned windows	~39%
energy-efficient appliances	~37%
insulation	~26%
HVAC	~26%
solar power	~22%
lower energy bill	~15%
high-efficiency water heater	~15%
water conservation	~10%
low- or no-VOC paint	~8%

KW RESEARCH

GREEN KEYS TO SUCCESS

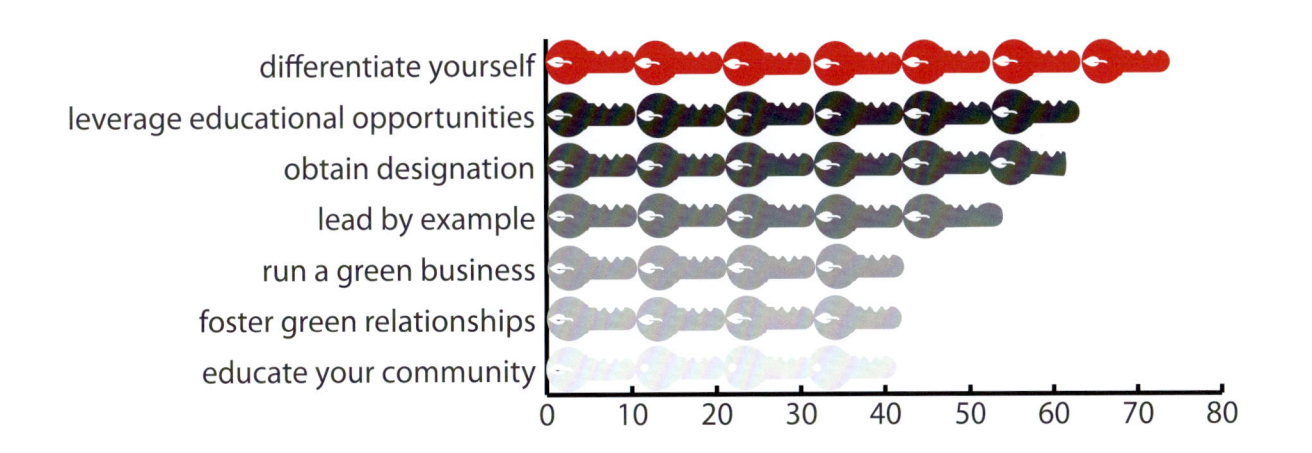

- differentiate yourself
- leverage educational opportunities
- obtain designation
- lead by example
- run a green business
- foster green relationships
- educate your community

0 10 20 30 40 50 60 70 80

8. GREEN IS THE NEW GOLD

SEIZE THE OPPORTUNITY: SPECIALIZED TRAINING

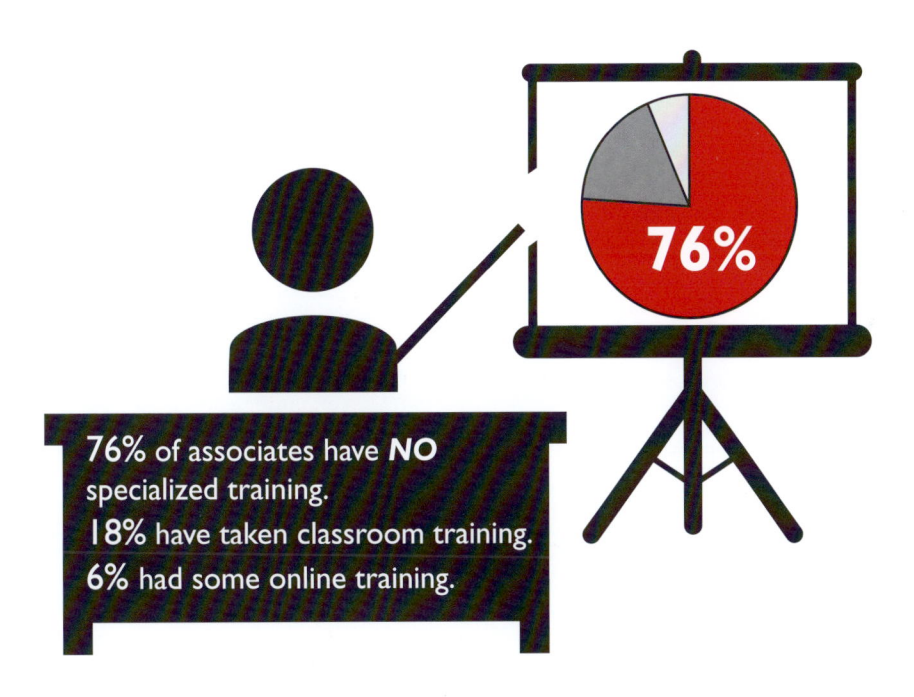

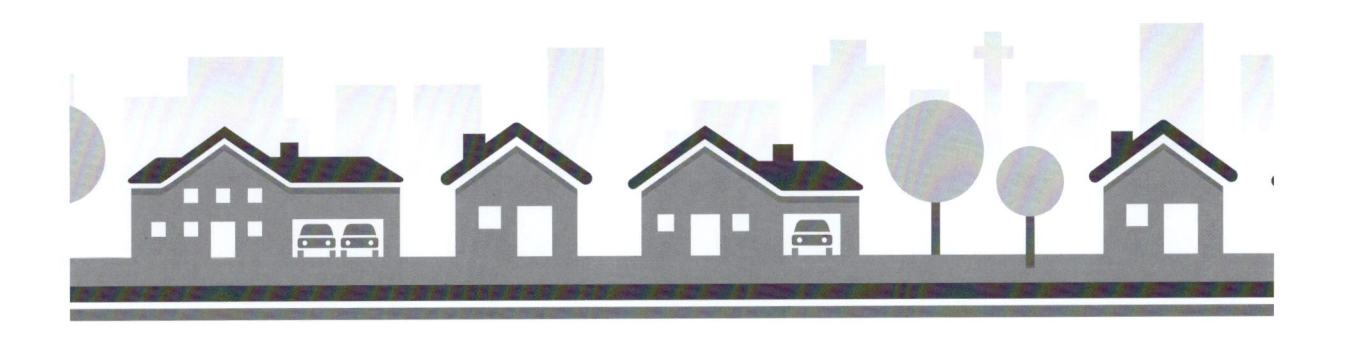

76%

76% of associates have **NO** specialized training.
18% have taken classroom training.
6% had some online training.

97

Lead Generation

Goals for Weekly Contacts 100

How Much Time Do You Block Each Week?.........101

Lead Generation Time Blocking............................101

Use of Traditional Lead Generation Sources.......102

Communication Preferences 102

Texting Is the New Email 103

Top Three Prospecting-Based Lead Sources........104

Top Three Lead Sources 105

Top Three Technology-Based Lead Sources.........105

Met Database 106

Haven't Met Database..106

Attracting Website Leads 107

Capturing Website Leads 108

Lead Generation

In order to survive, every business needs leads, and it is your job as a business owner to get them. While there are many methods of lead generation, ranging from door knocking to the latest social media, our research shows that two fundamentals are at the foundation of success: goal setting and effective time blocking that will enable you to achieve consistent results.

GOALS FOR WEEKLY CONTACTS

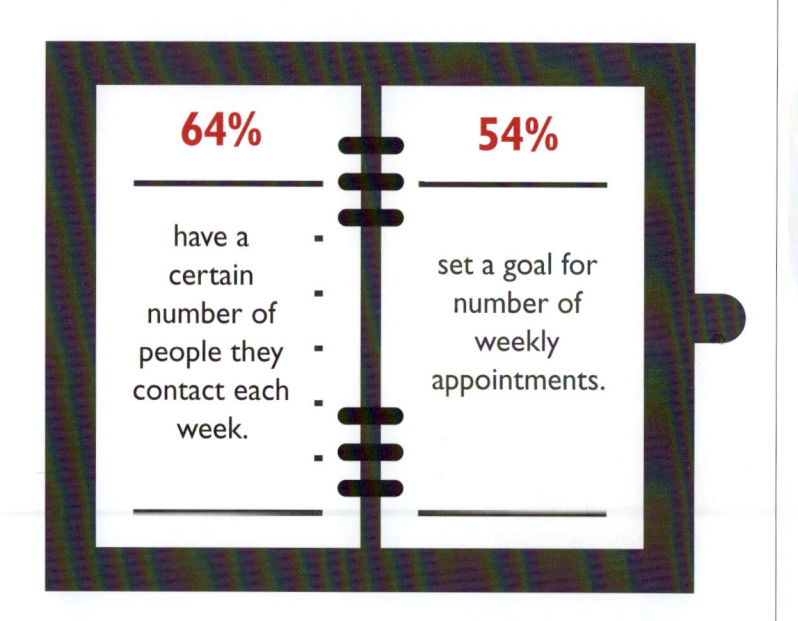

64% have a certain number of people they contact each week.

54% set a goal for number of weekly appointments.

58% practice scripts and/or dialogues with a colleague.

"When you are not practicing, remember, someone somewhere is practicing; and when you meet him, he will win."

Ed McCauley
Pro Basketball Player

KW RESEARCH

HOW MUCH TIME DO YOU BLOCK EACH WEEK?

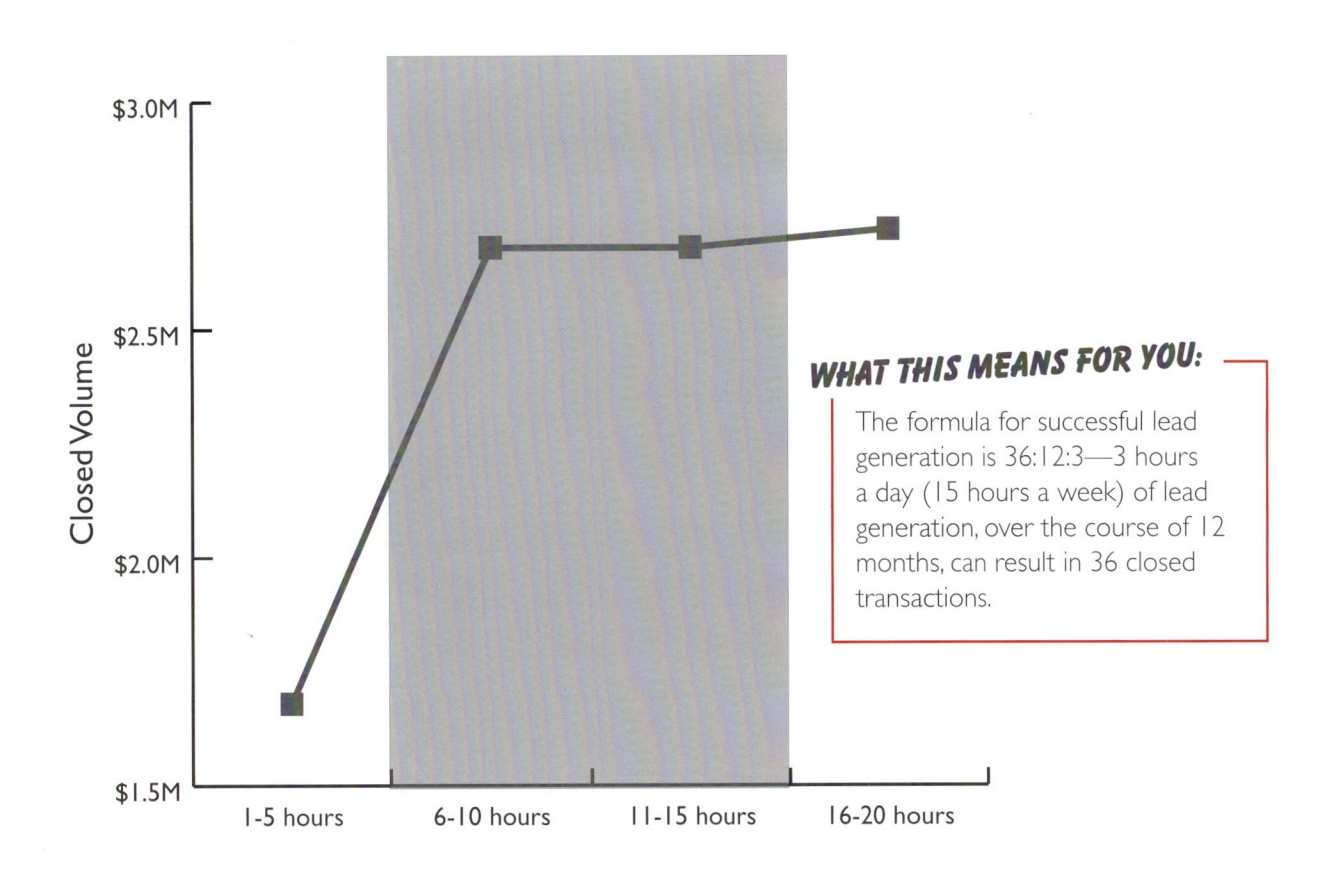

WHAT THIS MEANS FOR YOU:

The formula for successful lead generation is 36:12:3—3 hours a day (15 hours a week) of lead generation, over the course of 12 months, can result in 36 closed transactions.

LEAD GENERATION TIME BLOCKING

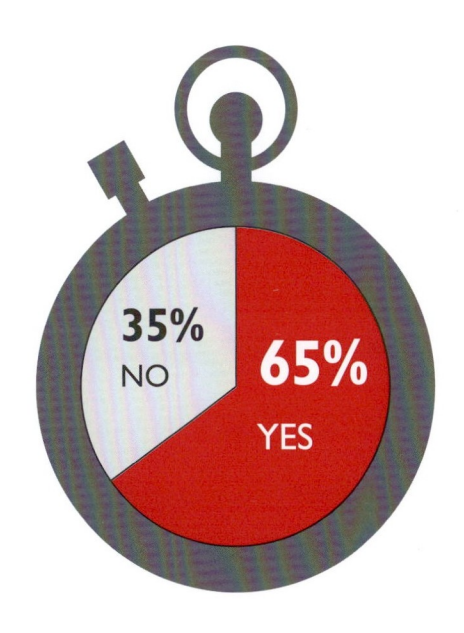

35% NO

65% YES

101

USE OF TRADITIONAL LEAD GENERATION SOURCES

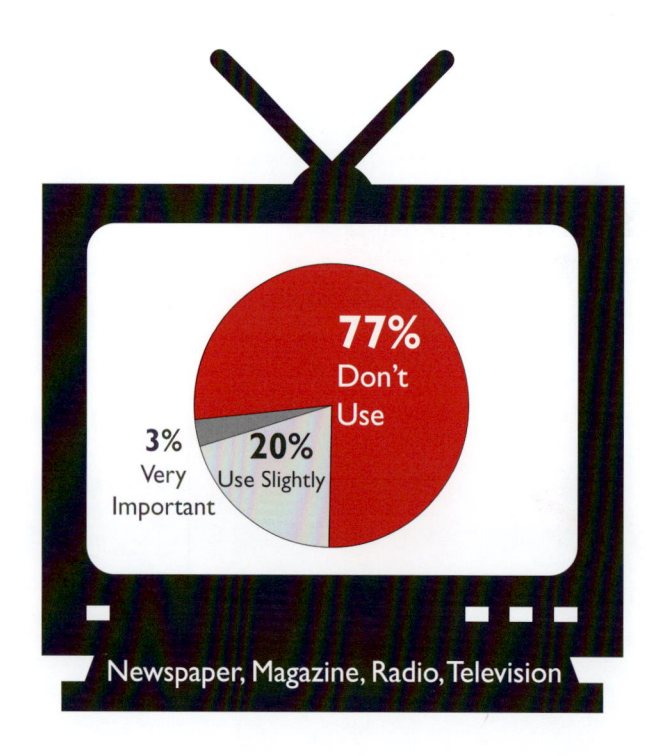

77% Don't Use
3% Very Important
20% Use Slightly

Newspaper, Magazine, Radio, Television

COMMUNICATION PREFERENCES

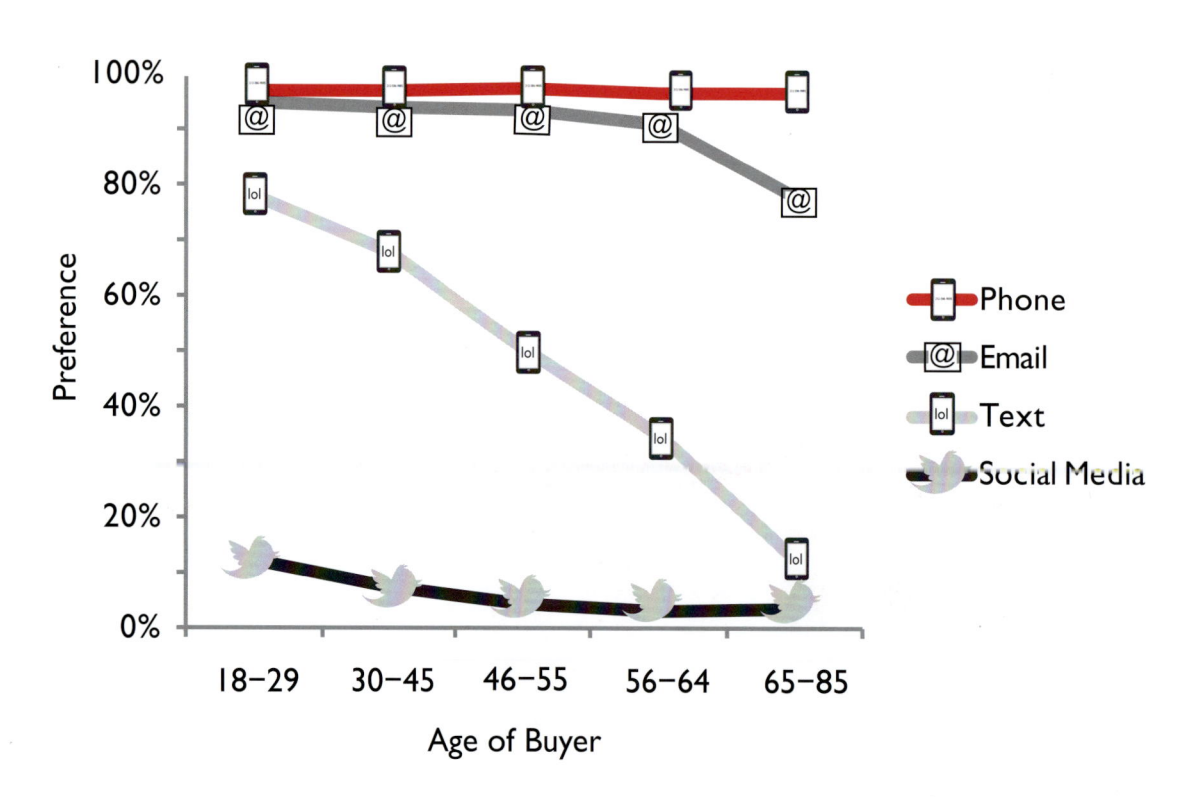

- Phone
- Email
- Text
- Social Media

Age of Buyer: 18–29, 30–45, 46–55, 56–64, 65–85

TEXTING IS THE NEW EMAIL

In last year's survey, 65% of those 30 years and under said that texting was their number one preferred method of communication. Just one year later, that percentage has climbed to 80%.

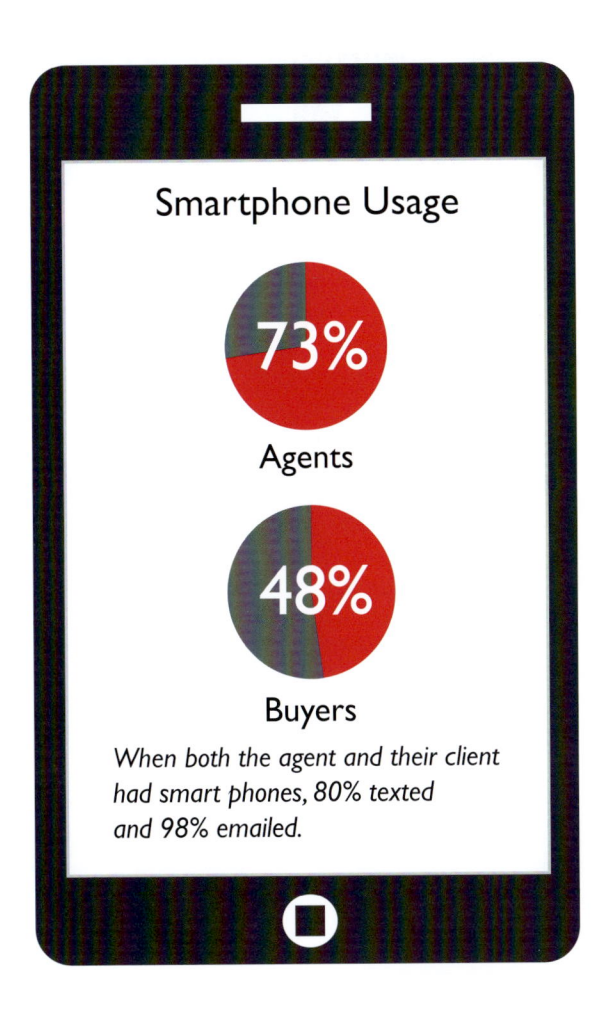

Smartphone Usage

73% Agents

48% Buyers

When both the agent and their client had smart phones, 80% texted and 98% emailed.

WHAT THIS MEANS FOR YOU:

During the buyer consultation, be sure to ask your buyers what method of communication they prefer. Note that the younger they are, the more likely they are to text.

57% of buyers under the age of 45 use smartphones.

TOP THREE PROSPECTING-BASED LEAD SOURCES

1

67%
Calling the Met Database

WHAT THIS MEANS FOR YOU:
Metworking works! It's not surprising that the top three lead generation prospecting techniques are Met based. To learn more about working your Met Database, refer to *The Millionaire Real Estate Agent*.

2

48%
Networking in Community

3

38%
Mailing Materials to the Met Database

"If you are not working your database, you might as well have 'pretend agent' on your card."
— Gary Keller

KW RESEARCH

TOP THREE LEAD SOURCES

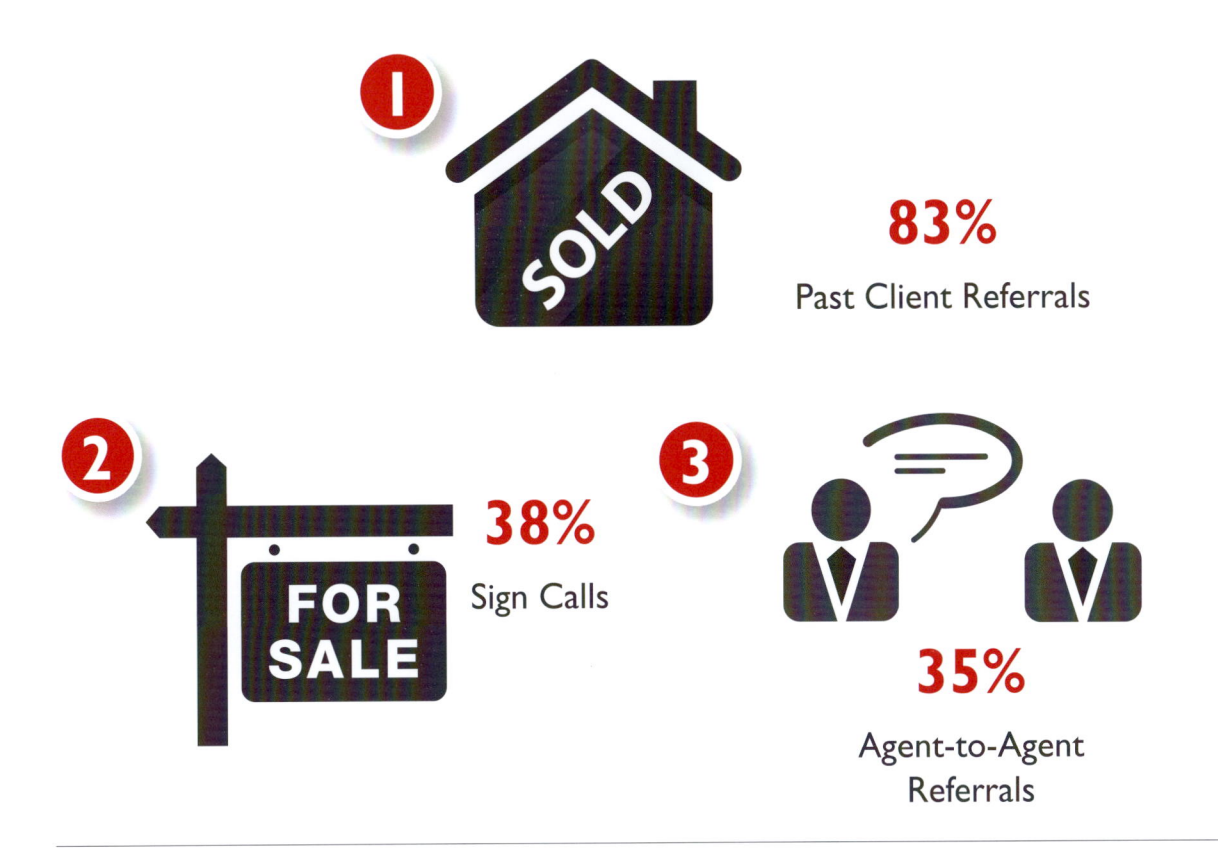

1 **83%** Past Client Referrals

2 **38%** Sign Calls

3 **35%** Agent-to-Agent Referrals

9. LEAD GENERATION

TOP THREE TECHNOLOGY-BASED LEAD SOURCES

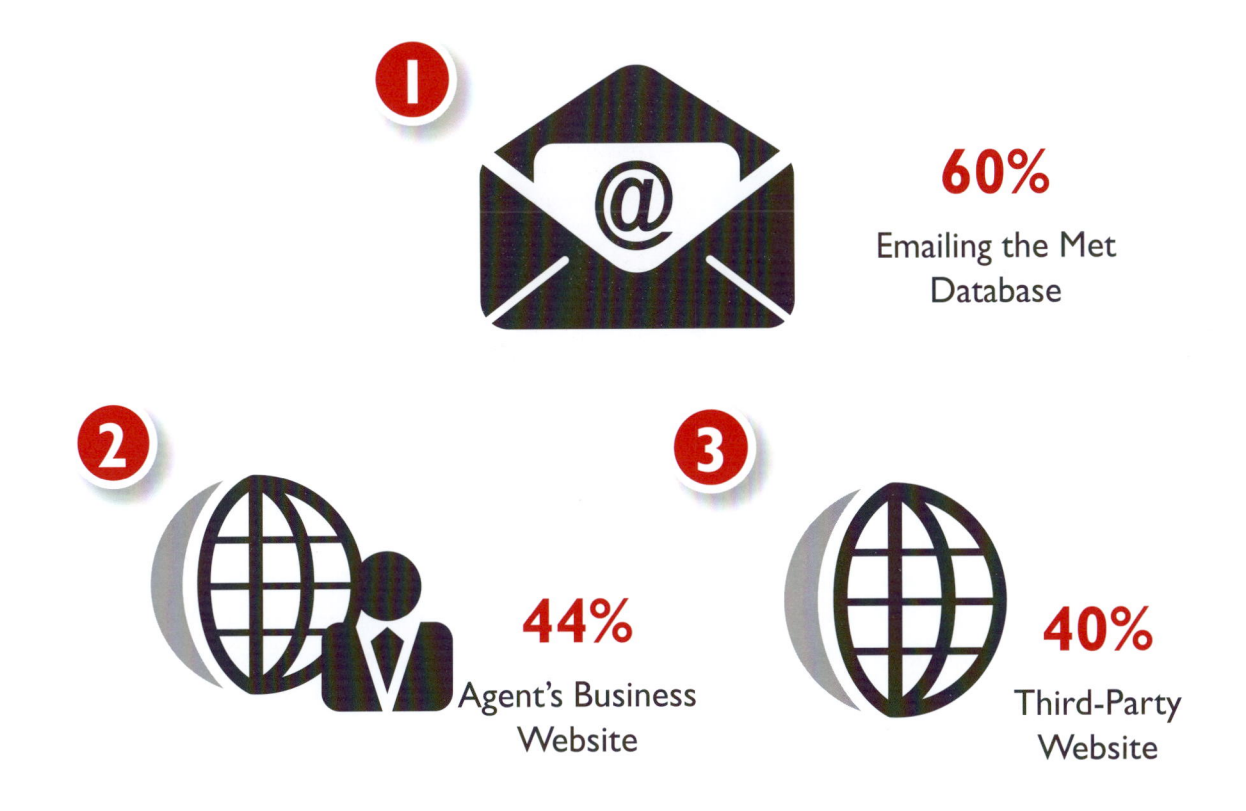

1 **60%** Emailing the Met Database

2 **44%** Agent's Business Website

3 **40%** Third-Party Website

MET DATABASE

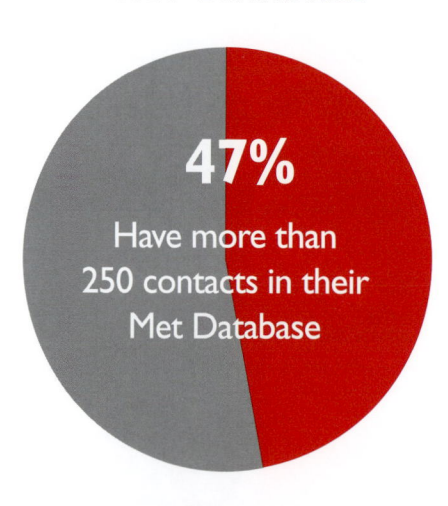

47%
Have more than 250 contacts in their Met Database

According to research conducted for *The Millionaire Real Estate Agent*, for every 12 people in your Met contact database to which you prospect and market yourself 33 times (33 Touch), you can reasonably expect to net 2 sales. Using a conversion rate of 12:2, to make 50 sales a year, you'll need to have 300 people in your Met Database who have gone through your 8 x 8 program and are in your 33 Touch program. While almost half of survey respondents are close to this minimum goal, you will join the ranks of an elite few if you exceed this number.

HAVEN'T MET DATABASE

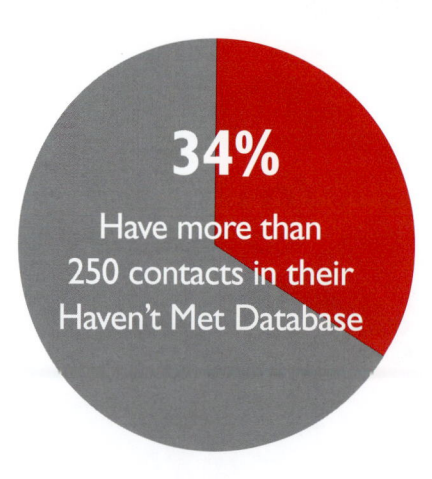

34%
Have more than 250 contacts in their Haven't Met Database

Working a large Haven't Met Database is a highly leveraged form of lead generation to the masses. Research in *The Millionaire Real Estate Agent* shows that for every fifty people you market yourself to twelve times a year, you can reasonably expect to hit an annual goal of 50 closed sales. At a 50:1 ratio, you'll have to have 2,500 people in your Haven't Met Database to hit an annual goal of 50 closed sales. The easiest way to hit this number is to actively work a farm.

ATTRACTING WEBSITE LEADS

87% capture more buyer than seller leads through their website.

5% of agents do not have a website.

734 average unique visitors to their website each month.

76% have a website which brings in leads.

26% get at least one-fifth of their leads from their website.

CAPTURING WEBSITE LEADS

"Contact me for more specific information on one of my listings" was the most compelling message to capture leads from the website.

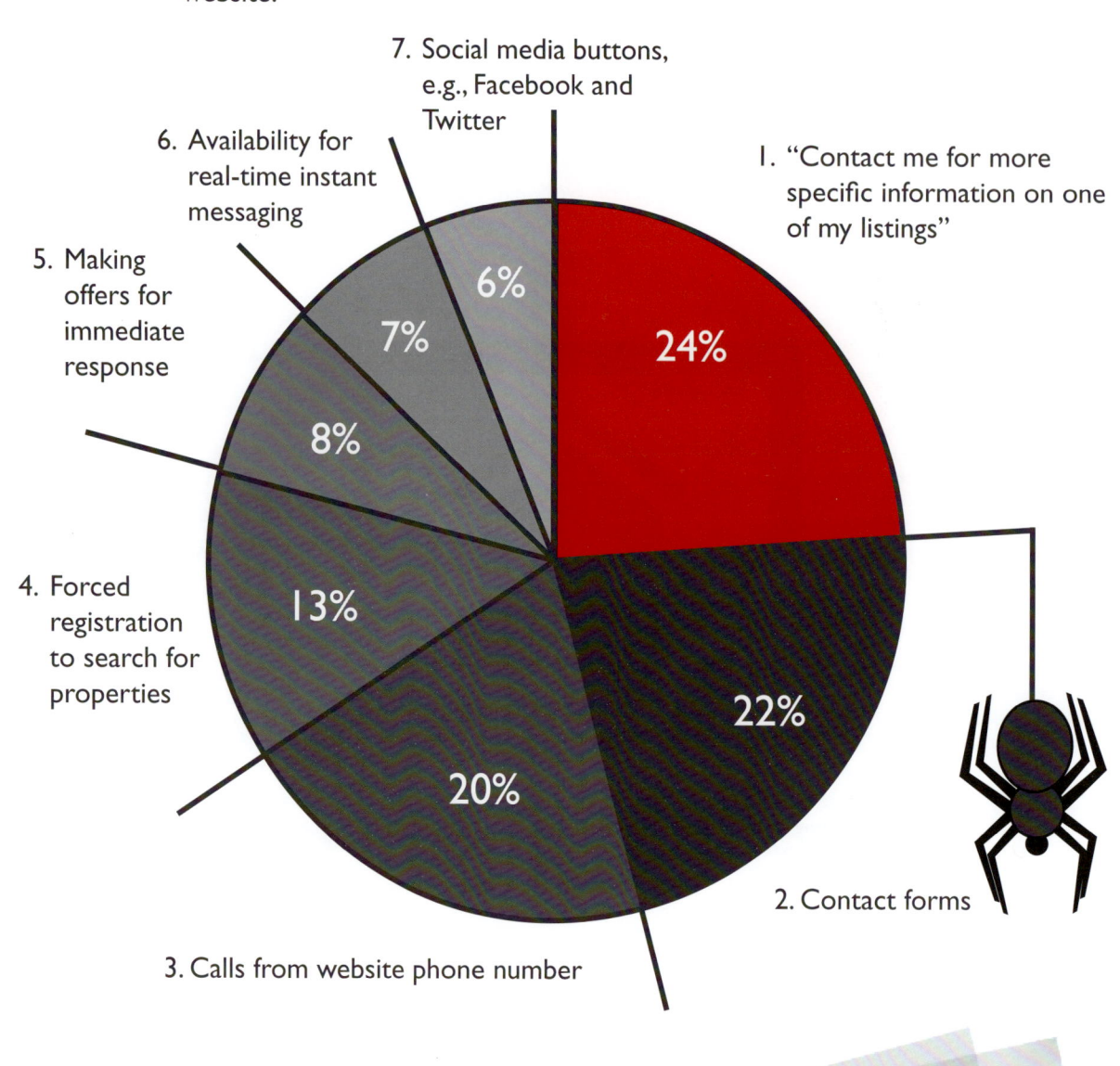

- 1. "Contact me for more specific information on one of my listings" — 24%
- 2. Contact forms — 22%
- 3. Calls from website phone number — 20%
- 4. Forced registration to search for properties — 13%
- 5. Making offers for immediate response — 8%
- 6. Availability for real-time instant messaging — 7%
- 7. Social media buttons, e.g., Facebook and Twitter — 6%

After obtaining contact information from an online prospect, 66% of agents contacted them at least five times and 25% contacted them at least eight times.

9. Lead Generation

Main Points

TOP 12 TAKEAWAYS

1. Homes are more affordable than ever.
    - Home prices have stabilized. They have yet to recover from the price drops caused by the market shift in 2007–2008. (Page 4)
    - Mortgage rates are at historical lows. (Page 6)
    - In 1981 if took 36% of the family income to pay a mortgage. Today it takes 14%. (Page 7)

2. It's a buyers' market, but inventory is trending downward, meaning that the golden age of buying will not last indefinitely. (Page 5)

3. Affordable pricing is the number one motivation for buyers, so it is no surprise that almost 1 in 3 first-time home buyers purchase distressed properties. (Page 57)
    - Good things come to those who wait. On average, buyers backed out of their contracts after almost 56 days, while the median wait time for an approval letter from the bank is 63 days! Counsel your distressed property buyers to be patient. (Page 83)

4. The top three three reasons home buyers want green features: (Page 94)
    - Energy Efficiency 80%
    - Long-Term Savings 66%
    - Better Indoor Air Quality 52%

5. Younger people (under 29) are the highest percentage of first-time home buyers. (Page 55)
    - Echo boomers are the fastest-growing segment in the workforce and are fueling growth just like the boomers before them. (Page 44)
    - 80% of those 30 and under are far more likely to use texting as their preferred means of communication. (Page 103)

6. Preapproval for buyers is the norm—64% of buyers get preapproved. (Page 50)

7. Buyer consultations set the stage for success. 91% of agents surveyed conducted buyer consultations to help streamline the buying process. (Page 49)

8. Pricing it right the first time can save sellers time and money. 48% of sellers priced their home according to their agent's recommendation (based on their interpretation of market value). (Page 73)

    - Those homes sold 49 days faster, in just 56 days compared to 105.
    - They sold for 6.7 percentage points higher in the list-to-sell ratio.
    - They sold with 1 less price reduction.

9. Condition is the key for serious home sellers. Homes in better condition sold for an average of 96% of the list price compared to homes in poorer condition which sold for an average of 92% of the list price. On a $200,000 home, that's a difference of $8,000. (Page 68)

    - The most common updates: (Page 67)
        - Paint 44%
        - Flooring 25%
        - Lighting Fixtures 20%

10. Staging is well worth the effort. The selling price of a staged house is typically 1.7% higher than an unstaged home. On a $200,000 home, that's a difference of $3,750. (Page 72)

11. Lead generation is the foundation for success in any market, and leveraging a healthy database is the method of choice. 67% of agents call their Met Database, and 83% rely on leads from past client to get referrals. (Pages 104 and 105)

12. Websites are a source of leads for 76% of agents. They average 734 unique visitors each month. The number one most popular message used to capture leads: "Contact me for more specific information on one of my listings." (Pages 107 and 108)

One of the things I know is that buyers and sellers in the marketplace expect you and me to provide them with **knowledge**, **expertise**, and **perspective**.

The best way for us to do that is to **spend some time with the numbers** so that we fully understand and appreciate where we are and where we have been.

Only then can we help people decide what they need to do in the future.

— *Gary Keller*
Cofounder and COB, Keller Williams Realty